EXPLANATION AND UNDERSTANDING
IN THE HUMAN SCIENCES

EXPLANATION AND UNDERSTANDING IN THE HUMAN SCIENCES

Third Edition

GURPREET MAHAJAN

OXFORD
UNIVERSITY PRESS

OXFORD
UNIVERSITY PRESS

Oxford University Press is a department of the University of Oxford.
It furthers the University's objective of excellence in research, scholarship,
and education by publishing worldwide. Oxford is a registered trademark of
Oxford University Press in the UK and in certain other countries

Published in India by
Oxford University Press
22 workspace, 2nd Floor, 1/22 Asaf Ali Road, New Delhi 110002

First Edition published by Oxford University Press in 1992
Oxford India Paperbacks, Second Edition 1997
Third Edition 2011

ISBN-13 (print edition): 978-0-19-807697-1
ISBN-10 (print edition): 0-19-807697-5

ISBN-13 (eBook): 978-0-19-908867-6
ISBN-10 (eBook): 0-19-908867-5

Typeset in 10/13 Palatino LT Std
by Excellent Laser Typesetter, Pitampura, Delhi 110 034
Printed in India by Repro India Limited

Contents

Acknowledgements

The work on which this book is based began in October 1980, and in the course of the decade my friends, acquaintances and family have been a constant source of strength, support and encouragement. To all of them I remain deeply indebted. Among the many who offered valuable advice, I would, in particular, like to thank Sarah Joseph and Sucheta Mahajan. Their readiness to listen, discuss and share research experiences saw me through many difficult patches. Niraja Gopal Jayal and Dipankar Gupta read several parts of the manuscript. To them I am grateful both for reading the dull prose and offering valuable suggestions.

I would also like to thank Bhiku Parekh and Nöel O'Sullivan for continuously subjecting my work to critical scrutiny. The questions they raised compelled me to clarify my ideas and to ground methodological issues in historical reality. I am, above all, grateful to Madhavan K. Palat, who supervised the Ph.D. thesis on which this work is based. Both the general argument and the detail gained a sharper focus under his critical gaze.*

To the Oxford University Press I owe an apology and a thank you: the former for my indiscipline, the latter for setting aside many deadlines. I hope the pages that follow might provide some justification for the long gestation period.†

* I am grateful to Satish Saberwal for meticulously reading the text and locating errors that had escaped even the professionals.

† As the Third Edition goes to press, I would like to take the opportunity to thank Nitasha Devasar for her initiative and assistance in bringing out this edition and the OUP team for taking care of the details efficiently.

Preface to the Third Edition

What is the nature of the social sciences? Are they significantly different from the natural sciences? Can social sciences offer complete explanations of social and historical reality? Do we need to rely on the methods of inquiry used in the natural sciences to arrive at objective knowledge of social reality? Does the study of social and historical objects—that is, things that are creations of the human spirit—require a different set of methods and frameworks of analyses? These questions structured not just the debates in the philosophy of the social sciences and history, but also the teaching of the social sciences in much of the twentieth century. Almost all graduate programmes began by examining these issues. Most often, they differentiated between the natural and the social sciences and then went on to identify the particular object studied in a given discipline, before examining the relationship between different disciplines that formed the rubric of the social sciences. This was the accepted and well-tried mode of introducing students to the social sciences.

Although these questions about the nature of the social sciences were a shared concern of social scientists, the answers to these questions varied significantly. While most social scientists differentiated the object of study in these two sets of disciplines,* there were important differences on the question of what was the appropriate method

---

* The natural sciences, it was said, analysed the external reality that existed independently of human beings, while the social sciences examined the 'objectifications of the human mind'. They focused on things that were, in the ultimate analysis, constituted by human beings and hence open to change.

of studying the social sciences and arriving at objective knowledge in these disciplines.

When I began working on this book in the 1980s, questions about the objectivity of social sciences inquiry and the scientificity of its knowledge claims dominated discussions in the philosophy of the social sciences. It was in this context that I attempted to emphasize the different ways in which the distinction between the natural and the social or the human sciences has been constituted and the different modes of inquiry that they have yielded. The primary consideration was to go bring into focus hermeneutic understanding and to show why explaining social phenomena by searching for causes or reasons for action is not always enough. Explanations are an important and integral part of the social sciences but at times it is equally essential to try and understand the difference or the specificity that defines the particular.

The idea that social sciences, or, as I explain in the book, the human sciences, must make space for plurality of methods, explanation, and understanding, is an element that needs to be emphasized strongly in the present context when students of social sciences rarely pause to consider the specific nature of their disciplines or that of the social or the human sciences. To some extent, questions about the nature of the social sciences and their knowledge claims became less urgent because the notion of science and objectivity that had defined the natural sciences, and which was the point of reference for differentiating between the natural and the social sciences, underwent considerable change by the end of the twentieth century. The criteria of complete confirmability and testability had given way to the notion of falsification, and more and more members of the scientific community came to accept that verification could not be the essential characteristic of scientific knowledge as it was an ongoing process—something that could in principle never be complete. These changes in the conception of science were accompanied by the understanding that observation of phenomena, whether natural or social, could not be completely independent of theory. Aspects that the knower must see and identify accurately to say that they have observed something, the experiments that the scientists design and what they infer from the results of these experiments, all entail interpretation.

The claim that theory or, what would be more accurate, theoretical paradigms, play a critical role in all forms of scientific inquiry and knowledge challenged the notion of objectivity and science that came initially from the Enlightenment and which was subsequently rearticulated by the Vienna Circle. It also weakened the need to examine and justify the nature of the social sciences or the objectivity of their claims. Once interpretation and the presence of theory was seen as a condition, rather than a limitation, in the pursuit of knowledge, features that were previously considered to be unique to the social sciences no longer appeared to be so. In effect, this meant that social scientists could go ahead and readily extend the methods of the natural sciences to their disciplines as the difference between the two appeared less stark; or else, keeping in mind the conditions of knowledge, philosophers of social sciences, along with philosophers of science, could seek alternatives to the prevalent conception of scientific method.

One would have assumed that in the time to come it would be the search for alternatives that would dominate the philosophy of social sciences. Indeed this seemed to be the case till the postmodern imagination moved from a critique of universalism and enlightenment rationality to the denouncement of the very engagement with method and discussions about objectivity and science. The space that opened with the postmodern critique of knowledge, truth and, more widely, foundationalism, has since come to be occupied by a new orientation and mode of engaging with the social reality—one which is marked by practical rather than theoretical considerations. The most striking illustration of this is that in lieu of existing disciplines, such as sociology, politics, and history, the study of the social is being re-conceptualized in terms of thematic entities. Poverty, development, environment, decentralization, social justice, and democracy, to name just a few, are being seen as issues around which the study of the social sciences should now be organized.

This re-organization of the study of the social is being reinforced by policy studies and the accompanying emphasis on outcomes and results. The common belief here is that subjects like poverty, development, and urbanization, for example, are compelling social concerns that confront developing societies the world over. To tackle the challenges that these societies face, the traditional study of social science disciplines is just not enough. What is needed instead is to bring together people from different disciplines and make them reflect upon and collectively engage with these issues. The assumption underlying this is that individual disciplines at best offer a partial analysis of the problems confronting us, and, in order to tackle the pressing issues of our times, such as poverty, development, and urbanization, a holistic approach is needed. It is, therefore, necessary to nurture scientific communities working on different problem domains, and along with it create the next generation that too focuses its energies on dealing with critical issues of our times.

In the mid-nineteenth century, Karl Marx observed that philosophers had so far only interpreted the world, the important thing was to change it. It is a cruel parody that in the era of neo-liberalism when even the welfare state is being pushed on the backfoot, advocates of policy-oriented studies are expressing their impatience with analyses and hoping to effect change by improving implementation and monitoring outcomes. Outcomes are, of course, important and we know that a brush with democracy enhances the expectations of individuals and groups for fair and equal treatment; it also makes citizens more impatient with the non-realization of this goal. Hence, it is not surprising that in democratic societies, even more than non-democratic societies, people want to see their governments devise policies that make a tangible difference to the quality of their lives. This widely-shared concern creates space for policy studies; indeed, in developing societies where the pace of change or improvement in life conditions is often slow, the need to monitor implementation of policies, and to measure results and check outcomes, gains a certain amount of urgency. But does this, and the concerns that arise around it, require a move away from the existing structure of the social sciences? Is it better and more desirable to divide the study of social reality around practical issues? These are questions that must be posed at this juncture.

To the policy analyst, focused on devising the 'right' policies that can yield the desired outcomes, an analysis of society aimed at explaining what happens, why it happens, or even efforts aimed at understanding what actually exists, often appears as an indulgence that must be set aside in the interest of finding solutions. But is this reasoning adequate? Are explanations, along with attempts at understanding the given reality, unnecessary for the task of addressing and solving the main problems of our time? Should subjects like poverty or development be considered as separate thematic wholes, each constituting an independent discipline of study?

To respond to these questions one must first recognize that almost all existing disciplines of social sciences serve, at least implicitly, a practical interest. Although knowledge is not pursued or valued with the sole intention of providing solutions to prevailing problems, nevertheless explaining and understanding the social world is informed by the belief that things can be, as Aristotle famously claimed, other than what they are. So objects that are now being proposed as independent and separate thematic wholes and disciplines—poverty, urbanization, democracy, and development—have received considerable attention in the different disciplines of the social sciences. The dissatisfaction with the existing analyses of these fields, therefore, rests upon the somewhat mistaken belief that each of these disciplines offers a partial view of these issues and problem domains. It is this notion that prompts some to argue for a new disciplinary structure that can give a holistic picture of the concerned issue by bringing together the findings and perspectives from different disciplines.

Looking at the manner in which disciplines of social sciences have evolved and the specialized body of knowledge that they have produced, there is indeed a tendency to engage with ideas and theories that have been produced within a given discipline. This is not to say that members of different disciplines are not aware of the writings that come from other disciplines; but as each discipline equips and trains its members in certain methodologies and intellectual categories, the tendency is to bring one's understanding and analysis to the refinement of these categories. So there is, perhaps, a need to create forums that bring together individuals from different disciplines. However, it must be kept in mind that facilitating exchange of ideas does not imply that different disciplines offer a partial picture of the reality, or that ideas or knowledge claims that come from different disciplines can be aggregated to constitute a single whole or complete truth.

The different disciplines of social sciences not only focus on different dimensions of the social reality, they also constitute their objects differently. Like Kuhn's paradigms they initiate us into asking and exploring a set of questions and simultaneously offer some theoretical and methodological tools, concepts, and categories, through which the given reality may be analysed. To put it in another way, it is not that economics focuses on the sphere of production and distribution of material goods, sociology the study of social institutions like family, and politics on the study of state and government alone; different disciplines tend to conceive the same object differently. If some view poverty to be a matter of income distribution, others see it as a dimension of class and status. They look at the same problem domain in diverse ways. It is this plurality, yielded through the plurality of disciplines, which offers a valuable resource for re-conceptualizing a problem or object of analysis—an element that is crucial for critically examining existing policies and programmes.

We could dispense with the plurality of disciplines and consider the knowledge being produced currently in the social sciences as irrelevant (or of little use) only if we operate with certitudes. It is not, therefore, surprising that voices that speak for the reorganization of social science disciplines along the lines of significant concerns and issues primarily find problems with the modalities of implementation of policies, and it is this sphere that receives their close attention. If the desired results are not achieved, for instance, if poverty persists or school drop-out rates do not decline, then it is assumed that the fault lies in the existing programmes through which the projected goals are to be realized. In other words, when the plea is made for orienting students to the study of such issues as development, poverty, urbanization, and exclusion, it is assumed that the ends are given and universally accepted and the only issue relates to the means chosen for realizing these ends or goals. Typically, the attempt in each of the existing disciplines of social sciences is to explain the given reality so as to put a question mark against the choices we have made: to ask, for instance, if the task is to increase agricultural production or create employment avenues; whether poverty can be minimized or tackled by increasing growth/production, or by offering vouchers for free meals or raising the levels of literacy. In other words, unlike the new trends in policy studies the different disciplines of social sciences critically reflect on goals as well as the options available for pursuing a chosen goal. They grapple with, and live with, doubts, questions, and uncertainties and not certitudes, and it is this that paves the way for re-conceptualizing our concerns, agendas, and, with it, policies as well as programmes for the implementation of those policies.

Before we arrive at solutions to the problems that confront our society we must analyse and understand the given social reality. We need to know why, for instance, poverty persists despite higher growth rates; why parents send their children to one kind of school rather than another; why girls join the social sciences stream rather than engineering in larger numbers. Explanations are needed to know how specific variables are related to each other; to see whether (to take another example) investments in the social sector result in higher rates of growth or if they follow after a certain level of growth has been achieved. Theories enter into the picture here: they suggest which variables might be linked together, and how we might test or observe the stipulated relationships. As each theory points to connections and relationships that were previously neglected, they contribute to the growth of knowledge.

The existing structure of disciplines and modes of drawing boundaries was the outcome of a specific historical process, and for this reason it may well change. The emergence of new theoretical frameworks and categories may incline us towards new ways of drawing boundaries, but the driving force for this change must be a new theoretical paradigm and with it intellectual categories rather than shared concerns, issues, or themes. When we are dealing with the social world, it is our capacity to see the given problem domain as part of a larger whole and in relationship with other spheres of that totality that creates space for critique and the articulation of difference. And it is this capacity that must be nurtured in the interest of human well-being.

Just as the availability of different disciplinary frameworks and theories contributes to our capacity to engage with the problems that confront us, so do the different modes of inquiry enhance our understanding of reality. If the causal mode of explanation helps us to explore why revolutions occur and de-centralization promotes stability, the hermeneutic mode of understanding prompts us to consider the different meanings that get inscribed into specific concepts in particular contexts. It adds to our analysis by compelling us to examine not just the causes for the lack of development, but also what a community considers to be development or human flourishing. If we are to deal with the problems of our times, we need more than just narratives of how certain tasks were accomplished by particular societies; we need to know why specific changes occur, what impedes or accelerates them as well as what kinds of change are desired and valued in a society.

As this book examines the different ways in which social scientists explain and understand the given reality, it will, I hope, also show why we need to nurture plurality of theoretical frameworks, disciplinary orientations along with plural modes of inquiry, and recognize that our engagement with the present is likely to be marked by differences and doubts rather than certainty and consensus. Perhaps the one thing that has emerged from our present engagement with the social sciences is that one must be cautious, if not wary, of attempts to brush aside the deep theoretical and methodological differences that mark the different disciplines of social sciences in the interest of mere problem solving.

May 2011

Preface

The agenda for the philosophy of social sciences was set, in the twentieth century, by positivism. For more than half a century it addressed issues that emerged from the positivist conception of science. While most philosophers and social scientists defended the scientificity of the social sciences, they did so in different ways. Some developed and perfected techniques of quantitative data analysis, others maintained that the nature of the object in the social sciences necessitated certain changes in the conception of explanation, prediction, laws, neutrality and objectivity. Within the Anglo-Saxon tradition few questioned the belief that social scientists *explain* the given phenomenon: they provide causal explanations of what happened and why it happened. To put it somewhat differently, most philosophers of social science accepted the notion of empirical validation, correspondence, objectivity and universality that informed positivism. What they argued against was the belief that scientific analysis involved a value-free and systematic collection of *raw* facts. Like most post-empiricist philosophers of science, they referred to the role of the subject in the cognitive process and acknowledged the presence of theory at different moments of the investigative process. The writings of Karl Popper and Thomas Kuhn reassured them that things were not very different in the natural sciences. Indeed, the writings of Kuhn were used to strengthen the claim that the difference between the natural and the social sciences was one of 'degree' not 'kind'. The natural sciences were marked by long periods of 'normal science' when the dominance of a given paradigm was not challenged by members of the scientific community. Periods of 'abnormal science'—where several paradigms coexist and compete with one another for dominance and control—were, relatively speaking, short-lived and far-between. The social sciences were different only to the extent that they had not arrived at the paradigmatic stage of normal science; that is, they were characterized by unending conflicts between competing paradigms. Several sociologists did, however, challenge this claim. They maintained that with the advent of Functionalism their discipline entered a period of normal science. Even so, most other social scientists offered sociological explanations for the inability of their disciplines to progress to the phase of normal science.

The desirability of ushering in an era of normal science had been questioned by philosophers of science, most notably Feyerabend, but social scientists were reluctant to endorse those conclusions because of their relativist underpinnings. Since paradigms are incommensurable and the world appears different to people using different paradigms, the coexistence of several paradigms would, in their view, entail the existence of so many different and heterogeneous worlds. And since our conception of the structure of the world was determined and shaped by the paradigm we use, we could not adjudicate between contending perceptions and claims about the nature and structure of the world. Consequently, they feared that in considering the coexistence of several paradigms as a desirable state, they would be abandoning the very idea of objectivity, truth and scientificity. Informed with this understanding only a few theorists pursued their arguments to their logical conclusion. While they accepted that the theoretical framework used by the scientist plays a crucial role in the collection and interpretation of data, they continued to endorse the correspondence theory of truth and maintained that hypotheses could be conclusively falsified on the basis of empirically collected data. Ignoring the fact that falsification of a theory is premised on the decisions of the scientific community rather than on the availability of a counterinstance, they merely redefined and rehabilitated the concepts of positivist discourse. In one form or another they continued to associate scientific inquiry with causal forms of explanation.

Causal explanations were, however, challenged by historians who emphasized the role of human agency in the historical process. In their view, historical events could not be explained merely in terms of the prevailing economic and political conditions; minimally, they required a reference to the actions of individuals and groups. To cite a couple of examples: the occurrence of the Russian Revolution could not be explained in terms of the developments in the economic and political sphere. The actions of the Bolsheviks made a crucial difference to the actual historical outcome. Similarly, the non-occurrence of the revolution in the advanced capitalist societies could not be completely explained by the developments in the mode of production. In each instance, a causal analysis of the existing situation needed to be supplemented by an analysis of the prevalent modes of consciousness.

Studies that examined the different ways in which subjectivity is constituted, typified and expressed in different societies brought into prominence new modes of explanation and understanding: they legitimized and gave currency to a new vocabulary and language of discourse. Social scientists began to refer to the object of analysis as a 'text' and maintained that occurrences in the historical world could be analysed and understood in the way in which we make sense of a piece of literary writing. Philosophers of social science, accordingly, analysed the nature of texts and reconstructed traditions that had previously been ignored in the Anglo-Saxon tradition. Hermeneutics became a byword symbolizing the displacement, if not a complete rejection, of the causal mode of inquiry and, with it, every form of positivism.

Just when it is becoming increasingly fashionable to use the metaphor of sign and signification, marginality and supplementarity, it is necessary to pause and consider the world signified in the new language: to see if the language of reading and interpreting a text entails a rejection of the causal form of explanation. In any case, before we rush to abandon causal language and idiom we need to re-examine the causal mode of perceiving and explaining the given reality, to see the kinds of questions it addresses, and to determine whether these questions can be accommodated in the new framework of analysis. The current work stems from these concerns. It presents reason-action explanation, hermeneutic understanding and the narrative as three alternatives to the causal mode of inquiry that has, in some form or the other, dominated the social sciences for several decades. As it specifies the distinctiveness of each mode of inquiry, it analyses the implications of using a particular vocabulary and language. More significantly, it examines whether the language of text and interpretation constitutes a separate mode of explanation and understanding, and whether the new language and the world-view expressed in it can be accommodated with other non-causal forms of explanation.

For the purpose of this study, the hermeneutic mode of understanding has been taken as an example of the new concerns that characterize contemporary writings in history and other human sciences. Conceived of as a specific method of recovering the meaning of a text, it has been placed alongside other modes of explanation and treated as *one* of the several non-causal forms of explanation. Long before the rediscovery of hermeneutic philosophy, historians had presented the narrative, and sometimes even reason-action explanation, as alternatives to the covering law model. Taking cognizance of the issues raised in that debate, this study perceives the hermeneutic mode to be another alternative to the causal form of explanation. To put it differently, it accepts that hermeneutic philosophy provided a conception of scientificity and objectivity that challenged the prevalent discourse on method. Apart from emphasizing the element of interpretation it offered a conception of historicity that had no place even in the post-empiricist conceptions of science. Hence, it did more than challenge the causal form of explanation: it altered the terms of the debate in the philosophy of social sciences. Nevertheless, we need not think of it as a negation of all other non-causal forms of inquiry. Indeed, it would be argued that the conception of man and history that informs hermeneutic understanding is compatible with the narrative mode. Even though the latter does not endeavour to recover the meaning of a text it can be informed by hermeneutic philosophy. While making this argument, one has redefined the notion of narrative. It is no longer seen as a chronological presentation of events one-after-another, or as a story with a beginning-middle-end structure; it is conceived of instead as a mode of configuration, and the difference is, to my mind, significant for any conclusions that we may draw about the adequacy of that mode of explanation for the human sciences.

Although it is customary to refer to the disciplines being analysed in this text as the social sciences, I have frequently preferred the term human sciences or *Geisteswissenschaften*. The choice has been dictated by three considerations: (i) literally, the term human sciences implies the systematic study of the creations and products of the human spirit.

By describing the object of analysis as an entity that is created and constituted by human beings, individually or collectively, it draws attention to the point that the object is not a mere fact given in physical perception; it is something that is *constituted* by humankind. The term 'social sciences' pushes this attribute of the object into the background. It highlights instead the collective and social element of the human enterprise. (ii) Within the social sciences we can envisage different disciplines, each analysing a particular dimension—e.g., political, economic, social, cultural, etc.—of the collective human enterprise. Since some activities are better organized and regulated and have a more enduring structure, it appears that the object of analysis and, correspondingly, the methodological concerns of the various disciplines are quite distinct. The human sciences, on the other hand, differentiate only between those objects that are constituted by men and those that are not. This conception, that stresses the similarities rather than the differences internal to a category, seemed more appropriate for arguing that the methodological issues discussed here are relevant for all disciplines that analyse objects which are constructed and constituted by men. (iii) Debates in the Anglo-Saxon tradition have been obsessed with the question of facts, values, relativism and objectivity. To move away from these concerns and to discuss questions pertaining to the suitability of a particular mode of inquiry for a given object, it seemed apt to lean on the German tradition and to recall the debate within which this question had been first raised. Way back in the mid eighteenth century, Chladenius, Wegelin, Gatterer and Herder had differentiated the logic and method of historical inquiry from that of mathematics and the natural sciences and argued that the former warranted a separate mode of inquiry. History, according to Wegelin, analysed the mutable and semi-free products of the human spirit—values, morals, opinions and social conventions— which cannot be apprehended mechanically in the form of cause and effect relationships. Consequently, while referring to the entire gamut of social, economic and political forces that operate outside, we need to refer to the motives and intentions of the agents. And the latter, Herder maintained, were aspects that can be known from the 'inside' by reconstructing the 'spirit of the age'. This book takes its cue from the writings of these theorists. It begins with the assumption that there are different ways of explaining and accounting for a particular occurrence, but it examines critically the accompanying belief that causal explanations are suitable for the natural sciences and Understanding for the human sciences. Questioning the search for a particular mode of inquiry that is adequate for the *Geisteswissenschaften*, it suggests that different modes of explanation conceive the object differently. When we choose a particular mode of explanation or understanding, we construct the object differently. Consequently, while discussing the adequacy of a particular mode of investigation, we need to dwell on just this aspect: we need to see how the object is being conceived of in that framework because that alone furnishes us with the grounds for *contingently* privileging one mode over another.

I

Explaining Causally

A causal form of explanation is characterized by a 'What-causal' interrogative.[1] It asks: 'What causal condition(s) caused/will cause the effect E?' While establishing a causal connection, the investigator assumes that the observed event is a consequence of some other antecedent event or condition.[2] Consequently, he tries to identify a condition or a set of conditions whose presence was essential for the occurrence of that event, and whose absence would have necessarily entailed the absence of that event.[3] In other words, causal explanation sets out to show that a particular event E is a necessary outcome of the specified condition(s) C and that the presence of C is sufficient for the occurrence of E. Since C is a condition that is both 'necessary and sufficient'[4] for the occurrence of E, it follows that it is a condition that

---

[1] P. Achinstein, *The Nature of Explanation*, Oxford University Press, New York, 1983, p. 220.

[2] While elucidating the nature of causal connections, Hume spoke of the relationship between pairs of single events while John Stuart Mill argued that invariable sequence rarely subsists between an antecedent and a consequent *event*. Usually such a relationship operates between a consequent and the *sum of several antecedent conditions*, each of which is required for the production of the effect. Even in nature we do not, he argued, see one kind of event being followed by another. What we do see is an event/effect occurring regularly whenever a *complex set of conditions* is satisfied.

[3] 'From a determinate cause an effect follows of necessity and on the other hand if no determinate cause is granted, it is impossible that an effect should follow.' B. Spinoza, *Ethics*, J.M. Dent & Sons, London, 1963, Part I, Axiom III.

[4] John S. Mill, *Collected Works, Vol. VII: A System of Logic Ratiocinative and Inductive, Books I–III*, edited by J.M. Robson, University of Toronto Press, Toronto,

is temporally antecedent to and regularly associated with E.[5] However, constant conjunction and spatial contiguity are only the observable attributes of causation: they symbolize the necessary though not the sufficient condition for the existence of a causal connection.

In other words, regularity of association is indicative of the possibility of a causal connection but, by itself, it does not denote a causal linkage. In a serialization or a classification the antecedent and the subsequent do not represent a causal connection even though they are constantly associated with one another. For example, on a record one song follows another with unfailing regularity, yet the relationship between the first and the second song is not a causal one. Similarly, we find that lightning always precedes thunder but we cannot, on that basis alone, conclude that the former is the cause of the latter. It is entirely possible that the two events (in this instance, lightning and thunder) are collectively caused by a third and altogether different event; or that, different factors independently cause each of these events in quick succession such that we regularly observe effect E (lightning) being followed by effect E (thunder). Consequently, to establish a causal connection and to assert that C is the cause of E we need to refer to 'positive' and 'negative' instances, that is, instances where E occurred and those where E did not occur despite the existence of similar antecedent conditions.[6] However, reference to other similar or comparable instances (where the same event occurred and others where the same set of antecedent conditions prevailed but were not followed by the effect E) is only a minimal condition for undertak-

---

1978, Book III, pp. 323-34.

[5] Although the cause is generally considered to be a condition that precedes the effect, nevertheless, the time difference is not crucial for the definition of a cause as there are innumerable occasions when the cause and the effect occur simultaneously. Using the example of a leaf that is being fluttered by the wind, Taylor asserts that 'it would be quite erroneous to say that the wind currents impinge upon the leaf and then, *some time later*, the leaf flutters in response'. Similarly, it would be quite erroneous to say that the hand moves as I pen words and sentences on a paper. See R. Taylor, 'The Metaphysics of Causation', in E. Sosa (ed.), *Causation and Conditionals*, Oxford University Press, London, 1975, p. 40.

[6] F. Bacon, *Advancement of Learning, Novum Organum, New Atlantis*, William Benton Publisher, Chicago, 1952, pp. 108-28.

ing causal inquiry. To specify the cause of an event we need to combine 'The Method of Agreement' with 'The Method of Disagreement', that is, to study the particular event E and enumerate the conditions that preceded the occurrence of that event, and then examine whether similar conditions prevailed in other instances where E occurred; also whether conditions $C_1 \ldots C_n$ prevailed in other instances where the effect E did not occur. Only if the condition C_1 was present in all instances where E occurred and the only one absent when E did not occur can we conclude that it was a condition necessary and sufficient for the occurrence of E. For example, we can conclude that broken homes are the cause of drug addiction among the young if: (a) most of the teenagers taking drugs come from broken homes; (b) they started taking drugs only after the separation of their parents, and (c) other teenagers in that residential area, belonging to the same social strata but coming from secure homes, do not resort to drugs. Similarly, we can say that inner-party factionalism was the cause for the decline in the Congress vote in the North only if the decline in votes occurred in states where party leadership was split while there was no corresponding shift in the votes polled by the Congress in states where there was no inner-party factionalism. It is of course assumed that the situation prevailing in the different states analysed was similar and comparable, and that there were no significant occurrences which might have influenced the shift in votes in some of these states.

In other words, the analysis suggests that, all other things being equal, inner-party factionalism was the cause of the decline in the Congress vote.[7] To eliminate the possibility of other conditions causing the decline in votes, one would also need to determine whether the votes lost by Congress were polled by the leaders and supporters of the factions. If our analysis revealed that the Congress vote declined only in those states where the party was split into factions, and that

[7] Needless to say, causal analysis of this nature requires a considerable amount of empirical research. Indeed systematic analysis and collection of data is required even to establish a correlation between inner-party factionalism and the decline in Congress votes; and for performing this task the investigator needs to specify observable and measurable indices for the phenomenon analysed. In this case he would have to specify, in observable and quantifiable terms, just what would constitute a decline in votes and inner-party factionalism.

these states had nothing in common except this one feature, then we could conclude that inner-party factionalism was the *cause* of the decline of the Congress vote. However, if we find that in most of the states where the votes of the Congress had declined a regional party had emerged, and we know (on the basis of other studies) that the latter has often resulted in a decline in the votes of the Congress, then one can establish that the former rather than the latter was a *cause* that was more important for the given effect if: (a) variations in the cohesiveness of the party were more frequently associated with variations in the votes polled by it; (b) the frequency with which inner-party factionalism led to the loss of votes was greater than the frequency with which the emergence of a regional party had the same result; (c) the probability of the votes declining when the party was split was greater than the probability of the regional party producing the same result.[8] However, if we fail to establish the relative importance of one condition for the desired effect, we might suggest that both conditions jointly produced the effect. In other words, we might regard it as an instance of multiple determination. The cause of an event may be one or many, but what characterizes causal explanation is the belief that the cause and the effect are linked contingently through a law. The existence of such a law or exceptionless generalization is regarded as a precondition for the existence and affirmation of a necessary connection between the two variables. Indeed, it is on the basis of such laws that we, through the identified cause, explain the given phenomenon, predict what will happen when a set of conditions operate, and retroactively, on seeing E, deduce that C must have preceded it. Consequently, the search for laws is considered to be an indispensable part of causal investigation. Two kinds of arguments are adduced in support of this claim: first, causal assertions are implicit in and may be deduced from such laws; second, every causal assertion refers, at least

---

[8] The process is, of course, much more complex than what might appear from the example. One would not only have to analyse the possibility of regional parties producing the same effect but also rule out the possibility of any other condition (say, electoral alliances among the opposition parties, the caste identity of the party candidate) producing the same effect. This, then, is only an instance of how the method of agreement and disagreement are meant to be applied while identifying a causal condition.

implicitly, to one such general law and the stipulated causal connection is defensible only if the corresponding general law is defensible.[9] The advocates of scientific history and the early positivists emphasized the need to discover laws of temporal succession and laws of coexistence inductively, through a careful and systematic collection of facts.[10] While the former iterated the need to begin with facts, the latter argued that a scientific theory must be reducible to basic sentences.[11]

[9] For example, we can accept that the epidemic was the cause of the decimation of the population only if the corresponding general law—'Under conditions $C_1 \ldots C_n$, whenever epidemics occur, populations are completely wiped out' is valid.

[10] Within the empiricist framework, facts and values formed binary opposites. Values were considered to be creations of the human mind that are imposed on the external world by the knower. Hence, they signified the subjective, arbitrary and non-verifiable elements that must be purged from scientific analysis. Facts, on the other hand, represented objective entities that exist in the world outside independent of the knower. Existing 'out there' in the world they were given in observation and subject to empirical verification. Hence, they were the only reliable building blocks of a scientific theory and analysis.

This conception of the fact-value dichotomy has since been questioned. Following Weber, most theorists make a distinction between value reference and value judgement and argue that the former is unavoidable even in the study of the natural phenomena. The choice of the object of inquiry, even in the natural sciences, reflects the individual, social or historical bias of the investigator. However, once the initial choice has been made the investigator becomes the 'servant of his evidence of which he will or should ask no question until he has absorbed what it says'. G.R. Elton, *The Practice of History*, Sydney University Press, Methuen & Co., London, 1967, p. 62. Also see M. Weber, *The Methodology of Social Sciences*, edited by Shils and Finch, Free Press, New York, 1968, p. 72.

[11] Basic sentences are those that represent pieces of information that are basic in so far as they are given in direct observation. For example, *I* feel hot. At 11.00 a.m., *I* am teaching in Room no. 101 of the New Social Science building, JNU. Each of these sentences refers to particulars and presents the experiences of an individual. As they are rendered indubitable by experience, they are incorrigible and akin to facts, i.e., statements about which one cannot be mistaken except in a verbal sense. This conception of basic sentences was subsequently criticized by Otto Neurath because it reduced scientific discourse to statements of individual and quite subjective experience. Neurath argued that a scientific theory must be derived from and be reducible to protocol sentences which are given in the form of observation reports, and expressed in physicalist rather than phenomenalist language. That is, they should have no reference to *I*, *now*, and *here*; e.g., Time

Two claims were implicit in this statement: (a) we must use concepts that refer only to observable entities;[12] and (b) only those propositions that can be completely verified and completely confirmed can be considered to be true and scientific.[13]

The inductivist conception of science that informed empirical research and causal analysis posed a variety of problems. For example,

---

11.30 a.m. S says she was teaching in Room no. 101 of the new SSS building of JNU from 10.00 a.m. to 11.00 a.m. This report would need to be compared with the observation reports submitted by other individuals and only those that *cohere* with one another could be accepted as the basis of a scientific theory. The notion of coherence that was central to Neurath's analysis was subsequently challenged by Karl Popper. For a detailed discussion, see K. Popper, *The Logic of Scientific Discovery*, Hutchinson & Co., London, 1968, pp. 96–100. Also see J. Joergensen, *The Development of Logical Empiricism*, International Encyclopaedia of Unified Sciences, vol. II, no. 9, University of Chicago, 1951.

[12] Later positivists, however, allowed the use of theoretical terms (even though they did not refer to any directly observable substance) on the condition that the means of operationalizing them were specified and the 'correspondence rules' by which they could be translated into observational vocabulary were explicitly stated. The notion of correspondence rules, like most of the other concepts that formed a part of the positivist vocabulary, was revised in the course of the debates in the Philosophy of Science.

[13] The notion of verification central to the positivist discourse on science posed some difficulties. A statement—'All swans are white'—could be conclusively verified only if we could claim to have observed all swans, a task that is extremely difficult, if not impossible, to perform. Consequently, Rudolf Carnap suggested the criteria of *complete* confirmability and *complete* testability as the test of the scientificity of a proposition. He argued that a statement could be completely tested and confirmed only if it contained no general universal or existential assertion. We could, in most other cases, achieve a *high* degree of confirmation even on the basis of a few positive results provided they were the 'right' kind of results. Or else, we could achieve a *reasonable* degree of testability by betting one theory against another. Although what counts as winning a bet would be determined by a variety of factors—e.g., nature of the hypothesis, evidence used, etc.—the scientist could, nevertheless, maintain that a particular theory/hypothesis has been confirmed to a reasonable degree on the basis of specified observation sentences.

The shift from verification to confirmation represented a significant change in the discourse on science as it was based on the assumption that hypotheses are not generated in a vacuum; they exist only in the background of other previously accepted hypotheses. Consequently, confirmation necessarily implied, and was relative to, the rejection of a rival hypothesis.

it assumed that we could derive a generalization from the study of particulars. Critics pointed out that a generalization could not be made on the basis of a finite number of instances because it is exceedingly difficult to specify the quantity of evidence that is required to formulate a universal statement or to validate a proposition. Therefore, we must either accept that a generalization is true in this instance, or else, we would need to justify it *ad infinitum*. Besides, if laws were merely generalizations derived inductively through the aggregation of previously observed cases, then there would be little possibility of explaining an event because each new case would only further substantiate the law or provide evidence that might lead to the confirmation or rejection of the law. If all generalizations and laws have to be repeatedly tested and checked against reality at each successive moment, they cannot form the basis of establishing 'necessary and sufficient' (causal) relationships.

Recognizing these problems, later theorists argued that a scientific explanation is one in which the explanandum (the event to be explained) is derived logically from a set of initial conditions and general laws.[14] General laws may be universal or statistical in form[15] i.e., they

---

[14] In the words of Carl Hempel, a scientific explanation consists of:
    (1) a set of statements asserting the occurrence of certain events $C_1 \ldots C_n$, at certain times and places,
    (2) a statement of universal hypotheses, such that
        (a) the statements of both groups are reasonably and well confirmed by empirical evidence,
        (b) from the two groups of statements, the sentence asserting the occurrence of event E can be logically deduced.
    C. Hempel, 'The Function of Laws in History', in P. Gardiner, (ed.), *Theories of History*, The Free Press, New York, 1959, p. 345.

[15] A general law is 'a statement of universal conditional form which is capable of being confirmed or disconfirmed by suitable empirical findings'. (Ibid., p. 345.) The use of the term *law* instead of hypothesis suggests that the statement is well confirmed by available evidence. It must be noted that Hempel differentiates general laws from other (non-lawlike) universal conditionals. The former, unlike the latter, do not contain any qualitative predicates nor do they refer to any particular place or time. Universal conditionals such as: 'All members of the Greenbury school for 1974 are bald' do not therefore qualify as a general law because they refer only to a particular group and are unable to explain why 'Henry Smith is bald'. C. Hempel, *Aspects of Scientific Explanation and Other Essays in the*

may represent what will necessarily happen in all cases or denote the probability of an effect following certain conditions. If the law is universal we can derive the explanandum (the event E) logically from the explanans (operative general laws and their boundary conditions), but if the explanans contains a statistical law we can deduce the event only if the probability is close to one. 'Under constant pressure the volume of a gas is directly proportional to the temperature' represents a law of the deductive nomological type. It states precisely the exact changes that we expect to find in the volume of a gas whenever the temperature is altered under the specified conditions. 'The probability of a candidate belonging to caste C winning from Patna is 0.8, is a law of the inductive statistical type and it does not make an unqualified statement about the occurrence of a given event. It only suggests the probability of an effect following certain antecedent conditions. And in such case we can predict only if the probability is close to 1. If the probability of the candidate winning is 0.5, then there are equal chances of C winning or losing the election. Consequently, we cannot predict the event to come with any degree of certainty. Irrespective of the kind of law invoked in a particular instance, the subsumption of an event under a general law is regarded as the hallmark of a scientific explanation.[16]

Thus, both the inductive and the deductive conceptions of science endorse the use of general laws and argue that the efficacy and truth of an explanation rest on the veracity of the adduced general law. As the explanatory potential lies in the use of a general law, discovering and establishing laws of succession and coexistence are considered to be an important and indispensable part of scientific investigation. Since social scientists are unable to furnish such laws, Hempel argues that in these disciplines we do not find complete explanations. In history, for example, we only have explanation-sketches.[17] Historians

---

Philosophy of Science, The Free Press, New York, 1965, pp. 334–9.

[16] It is perhaps, for this reason, customary to refer to his conception of scientific method as the Covering Law model.

[17] C. Hempel, 'The Function of Laws in History', p. 351. Also see C. Hempel, 'The Logic of Functional Analysis', in M. Brodbeck, (ed.), Readings in the Philosophy of Social Science, Macmillan, New York, 1968.

use terms like 'because', 'therefore', 'hence', 'consequently' which indicate the use of a general law but they do not regard it as their task to establish these laws. In other words, explanations given by historians indicate in vague and rather imprecise terms the relevant law and initial conditions but each of these needs to be 'filled out', i.e., further research is required to enumerate completely the conditions $C_1 \ldots C_n$ that are necessary for the operation of the law, and to show that the conditions referred to in the explanation are actually relevant.[18]

The belief that every causal explanation refers at least to one general law and there can be no explanation without such a law has been challenged on two grounds. It is argued that social scientists, particularly historians, are concerned with the study of particular occurrences: they examine what happened in *this* particular instance (say, of famine or riot) and not what happens every time such events (famines and riots) occur. Consquently, they neither set out to establish general laws nor do they feel that a reference to such laws is adequate for explaining 'unique particulars'. Secondly, and more importantly, 'dredging up' the relevant law is *not* always necessary for explaining a given occurrence.[19] We may, for instance, say that this explosion was caused by the bomb in the closet without knowing what the relevant law is. Similarly, we may be completely ignorant of the relevant law when we explain our inability to light the fire by saying that the matches are wet. To put it somewhat differently, several theorists argue that the linking together of two variables or objects points to the existence of a law but an explicit reference to that law is not necessary for furnishing an adequate explanation. Thus they question Hempel's

---

[18] Cf., E. Nagel, 'Some Issues in the Logic of Historical Analysis', in P. Gardiner (ed.), 1959, p. 375; and E. Nagel, *The Structure of Science*, Routledge & Kegan Paul, London 1971, p. 550.

[19] To quote D. Davidson, 'It does not follow that we must be able to dredge up a law if we know a singular causal statement to be true; all that follows is that we know there must be a covering law . . . . Our justification for accepting a singular causal statement is that we have reason to believe an appropriate causal law exists, though we do not know what that is.' D. Davidson, 'Symposium: Causal Relations', *Journal of Philosophy*, vol. LXIV, no. 21, November 1967, p. 701. Also see C.J. Ducasse, 'Critique of Hume's Conception of Causality', *Journal of Philosophy*, vol. LXIII, no. 6, March 1966.

conclusion that historians and social scientists do not provide complete explanations, but they do not question the belief that every explanation refers, *at least implicitly*, to one general law. They merely defend the scientificity of these disciplines by rejecting the assertion that the primary task of a social scientist is to establish laws.

Even those who emphasize the study of concrete particulars merely argue that the stipulated causal condition applies (or can apply) only to the event under consideration; it cannot be regarded as the cause of all events similar to E. They do not also question the belief that a cause is related to the effect contingently through a law. Indeed they are more sensitive to the idea that the condition that makes the crucial difference depends, to a considerable extent, on the precise configuration of forces at that time, because the presence of other factors which appear to be insignificant individually may, in association with other factors and conditions, make a substantial difference to the outcome. Hence, it is not possible to explain all events similar to E by referring to the causal condition C nor is it possible to predict, from the presence of C, the precise nature and time for the occurrence of E.

The difficulty is further compounded by the fact that events in the social world do not repeat themselves. They may be similar but are rarely, if ever at all, identical. As such, to explain a *particular* occurrence it is extremely important for the social scientist to take cognizance of the precise differences. Reference to the general law is insufficient for another reason. General laws only suggest the *type* of event that might occur; they do not and cannot specify exactly what did happen. For the latter we need documentary evidence because a whole range of qualitatively different events, each of which satisfies the same general description, could have happened.[20]

It is important to reiterate that even these theorists do not question the existence of a law on the basis of which we can link a particular factor antecedent to the event with the consequent. They only question the belief that the covering law model provides a viable account of the structure of scientific explanation and argue instead that subsuming an event under a law is not sufficient because a variety of events can be subsumed under one law and almost any event can be subsumed

[20] For details, see chapter IV.

under a law. Consequently, they argue that the important thing is to see which condition is, or can be, related to a particular effect or which laws are invoked in the analysis. The latter is considered to be important because the covering law model does not provide any basis for determining the cause of an event. To cite an example given by Michael Scriven: if conditions present in a case at 4.00 p.m. guarantee a stroke at 4.45 p.m. and consequently death at 5.00 p.m., but an entirely unrelated heart attack occurs at 4.45 p.m. such that death occurs at 5.00 p.m., then, under the circumstances, the covering law model would be committed to both the stroke and the heart attack as explanations for each can be linked through a law to the actual event (death). Although it is the heart attack and not the stroke that should be called the cause, the covering law model does not provide any criterion by which we can exclude one of them.[21]

It is further argued that the notion of general law itself is quite ambiguous in Hempel's writings. He does not, for instance, provide a satisfactory way of distinguishing between general laws and other general conditional sentences, that is, between law-like universal conditionals and non-law-like universal conditionals. Given the premise: 'Henry Smith is a member of the Greenbury School Board' and the universal conditional: 'All members of the Greenbury School Board are bald', we can (in the manner of deductive nomological explanations) deduce that Henry Smith is bald. However, Hempel suggests that statements of this kind cannot be considered as general laws because law-like sentences must be of an 'essentially generalized' form: they must not contain any reference to particulars and should not be 'equivalent to some finite conjunction of singular sentences'. But these criteria given by Hempel do not rule out a sentence like 'All members of the G. School Board are bald' for it does not name the members of the School Board and is not therefore equivalent to a conjunction of singular sentences.[22] Nor can one object on the ground that it refers to a finite number of members because the criterion of

[21] M. Scriven, 'Critical Study of E. Nagel's The Structure of Science', in *Review of Metaphysics*, vol. XVII, no. 67, March 1964, pp. 410–11.

[22] See Edward J. Neill, 'Review of Carl G. Hempel's Aspects of Scientific Explanation and Other Essays in the Philosophy of Science', in *History and Theory*, vol. VII, 1968, pp. 231–2.

number is hardly adequate. Besides, laws are in general relative to what they explain and even in the natural sciences we have laws that refer to particular objects, time and location.

Setting aside the difficulties associated with the use of general laws for explaining an event causally, Hempel's analysis, we find, presents several other problems. It refers only to the structure of scientific explanation and does not take into account what scientists do when they explain a particular phenomenon. Nor does it analyse the form in which these explanations are actually presented by the scientists. Hempel maintains that his analysis is concerned only with the *logical* structure of scientific explanation and not with any given scientific practice, but this is itself a major limitation of the model. It is not therefore surprising that most social scientists and historians question this notion of scientific explanation on the ground that it is hardly ever used by them.

From the point of view of the social sciences, the most serious problem with Hempel's covering law model, as also with the conception of cause as a necessary and sufficient condition, is the belief that a successful prediction is an attribute of a scientific explanation, and that an explanation can be considered valid and scientific only if the event could have been predicted on the basis of the knowledge adduced explicitly in the explanation. Equating explanation with prediction, it ignores the fact that explanation and prediction are two separate activities involving two different kinds of evidence and knowledge. Prediction represents a special craft and a technique; it is an application rather than the kernel of science. It assumes the existence of a necessary and recurring sequence of events which is not essential for the operation of a causal relation. In order to predict we have to construct a universal proposition of the sort: 'whenever B also A'. For the latter we need to enumerate the circumstances in the absence of which B would not cause A and claim that the absence of B would necessarily imply the absence of A. Thus, for prediction we must not only specify the circumstances in which A comes from B but also assert that necessarily 'If B then A' and 'If not-B then not-A'. Only if not-B is a sufficient condition for not-A can we say that 'whenever B also A'.[23] Regularity of sequence, as we argued earlier, is relevant for

[23] Cf., G.E.M. Anscombe, 'Causality and Determination', in E. Sosa (ed.), 1975,

the meaning and operation of a law. It is important for the discovery of a causal connection, it does not define the notion of cause.[24] Prediction, on the other hand, assumes the principle of regularity and rests on the existence and application of general laws. The distinction between explanation and prediction is manifest in another way: we can sometimes make scientifically significant predictions that contain little or no explanatory force. On seeing dark clouds in the sky we may successfully predict rainfall but that does not constitute an explanation of the event (rainfall). Similarly, on seeing large crowds at a public meeting organized by party 'P' we may predict that its candidate will win the elections from that constituency. This prediction may subsequently come true but it would still not constitute an explanation for the success of the party's candidate in that area. In other words, on the basis of a few symptoms and indications we can, on several occasions, predict the event with a considerable degree of accuracy, but this does not constitute an explanation of the event. The opposite is equally true. On the basis of Darwin's theory of evolution, we may explain the emergence of a new species but it is exceedingly difficult, on the same basis, to predict with accuracy the specific form of the new species that will emerge.

Moreover, the assumed symmetry between explanation and prediction rests on the belief that the given object will function in the same manner and in accordance with known principles and laws. In other words, it presupposes the operation of the principle of regularity and is contingent upon the recurrence and repeatability of things. In a minimal sense these conditions cannot be fulfilled in the social sciences because these disciplines analyse the creations of human beings, and human beings do not always act in an invariable and repetitive manner. This introduces an element of uncertainty, consequently, even on the basis of a complete explanation we can only suggest what might

---

pp. 69–70; and O. Hellevik, *Introduction to Causal Analysis*, George Allen and Unwin, London, 1984, p. 25.

[24] M. Ginsberg, 'Causality in Social Science', *Proceedings of the Aristotelian Society*, New Series, vol. xxxv, 1934–5, p. 67. Also see C.J. Ducasse, 'On the Nature and Observability of the Causal Relation', in E. Sosa (ed.), 1975, p. 118.

happen: the success of these predictions cannot be ensured even theoretically. Since the inability to predict accurately stems from the nature of the social scientist's object of study, several philosophers of social science have redefined the notion of cause and the structure of causal explanations in a manner that would take cognizance of this difference.

The redefinition of cause was accompanied by the claim that the social scientist provides explanations of *particular* events rather than of *types* of events. When an investigator treats an event *e* as an instance of the event *E* then his causal assertion '*c* is the cause of *e*' implies that *c* is the cause of all events of the *type E*. However, when event *e* is not seen as an instance of an event of the type *E*, then the latter conclusion does not follow. In other words, in such cases it does not follow that *c* is the cause of all events of the type *E*; instead it is seen only as the cause of this event *e*. Consequently, such explanations render *singular causal assertions* rather than causal explanations of the earlier kind. The argument can be made slightly differently. When we say that the historian is not concerned with an analysis of why populations disappear, empires decline or colonies are freed but with the particular instance of 'Why the Minoan population was decimated', 'Why the Roman empire declined', 'Why the British left India', etc., we assume and suggest that the decline of the Roman empire can be explained quite differently from the decline of the Mughal empire and the decolonization of India explained differently from that of Malaysia. This does not, however, imply that different instances of the decline of empires or of decolonization have nothing in common; it only asserts that a reference to these common conditions is insufficient and inadequate for understanding the precise nature of that event. The emergence of the bourgeoisie may have been a condition that preceded the occurrence of both the French and the English revolution but by itself it cannot adequately explain the precise nature, form and consequences of each of these revolutions. Similarly, the existence of a powerful movement for national liberation may be a condition that precedes decolonization but, by itself, it cannot explain why the British decided to leave India in 1947. To explain the precise occurrence and to identify the condition that made the 'crucial difference' to the outcome, one needs to analyse the configuration of forces at that moment in time in that society.[25] One would, for instance, have to identify the complex of conditions that preceded the transfer of power in order to determine which of these in itself or in conjunction with others made the crucial difference and influenced the British decision to leave India by August 1947. In other words, based on the study of the determinate situation that prevailed at the time of this occurrence, one would have to specify the cause of this particular occurrence.

Singular causal assertions of this kind are regarded as a valid and legitimate form of inquiry that explain completely and adequately why something happened. Indeed, it is argued that they denote all that is entailed in a causal relationship. Like causal explanations they refer, explicitly or implicitly, to at least one law, the only significant difference being that the laws used in such explanations are complex, elliptical and only 'partly open'.[26] That is, they use laws or universal propositions that are incomplete and there may be other conjuncts and disjuncts of the law that are as yet unknown and need to be 'filled in' later.[27] In other cases the general law employed may have references to particulars, and hence, may apply only to the case at hand.

The acknowledged difference in the nature of general laws used has important implications for the notion of causal explanation. First and foremost, it dissociates explanation from prediction: if the laws are not completely open and do not refer to other instances of the same phenomenon, they cannot form the basis of predicting what will/must happen whenever C is present. The absence of predictive ability does not, however, affect the explanatory power of the assertion. Singular causal assertions, it is argued, provide a complete and non-prob-

---

[25] See Robert K. Shope, 'Explanation in Terms of "The Cause" ', *Journal of Philosophy*, vol. LXIV, no. 10, 1967, pp. 312–20.

[26] Historians do not say 'windows are brittle'; they assert that '*those* windows are brittle'. Similarly, they do not specify the conditions under which rulers declare war on neighbouring countries; they delineate the conditions under which a particular ruler declared war on a particular neighbour. Cf. Alan Donagan, 'Explanation in History', in P. Gardiner (ed.), 1959, p. 435.

[27] In the words of J.L. Mackie, 'whenever we have a singular causal statement we shall still have a covering law . . . albeit a more complex and perhaps an elliptical one'. J.L. Mackie, 'Causes and Conditions', in E. Sosa (ed.), 1975, p. 36.

abilistic explanation of an event *post factum*.[28] They explain fully why a particular event (say, the transfer of power to India in 1947) occurred by identifying a condition that was *necessary under the circumstances*.[29] Beginning with the assumption that the same effect could have been produced by some other condition, the advocates of this notion of cause emphasize the need to analyse the actual situation to determine which of the possible causal conditions was actually present at the time of the occurrence of this event. If, for instance, we know that the fire in the hall could have been caused by a shortcircuit or a gas leak, we would need to examine the situation preceding the fire to determine which of these was the cause under the operating circumstances. Similarly, on the basis of other studies, if we know that earthquakes and epidemics have resulted in the decimation of populations, one would have to see which of these conditions existed in this instance. If there is no evidence of an earthquake but the records show that there was an epidemic, we might safely presume that the latter was the cause for the decimation of the population. If we find that both the conditions—epidemic and earthquake—were present at short intervals, then the condition that intervened first would, under the circumstances, be the cause. The condition that intervened first would be the cause because we assume that condition C_1(epidemic) would have resulted in the effect E (decimation of the population) thereby making the later

[28] To quote an example: 'Suppose we had a gun that shot bullets through a force field at a screen, what is special about the force field is that it is composed of force vectors that change with time in a completely randomised fashion. So we cannot predict, in principle, where each individual bullet will arrive at the screen. However once each bullet makes it to the screen, we have a *post hoc* causal explanation as to its Y position . . . . This is a causal explanation of an individual event but it is not a probabilistic explanation at all. I am not saying that the bullet ended up there because it was very likely that it would. On the contrary it may have been very unlikely that it would arrive at that particular location on the screen; nevertheless, it ended up there because the field happened to deflect it there.' J.L. Aronson, *Realist Philosophy of Science*, Macmillan, London, 1984, pp. 64–5. Likewise, we may not be able to predict the migration of Dust Bowl workers to place P at time t_1 but once they migrate to P we can explain why they decided to migrate to P at that moment in time.

[29] See H.L.A. Hart and A.M. Honoré, *Causation in the Law*, Clarendon Press, Oxford, 1973.

condition C_2(earthquake) redundant and unnecessary for the effect under consideration, namely, the decimation of the population.

The identified cause, in this framework, is considered to be a condition that was contingently necessary or necessary under the circumstances; it is assumed that the same effect could be produced by another condition but, under the given circumstances, it is the presence of this condition (referred to as the cause) that brings about that effect. Further, the identified cause is a condition whose presence made the crucial difference such that the same result (effect) would not have followed if that condition was absent. While arguing that the identified condition was, under the circumstances, responsible for the given effect this conception of cause does not refer to other conditions in whose presence the causal condition produces the given effect. While identifying the epidemic as the cause of the decimation of the population it does not consider other conditions—for example, the absence of medical facilities—as being essential for the operation of the causal condition. Similarly, while identifying the presence of the lighted cigarette butt as the cause of the fire in the hall, it does not refer to the absence of the fire alarm system as an important conjunctive condition whose presence enabled the causal condition to produce the given effective conditions. It is only in the presence of the carpeted floor (X), an inflammable substance (Y) and the absence of a fire alarm system $(\bar{Z})$ that the lighted cigarette butt on the floor causes the fire in the hall. The lighted cigarette butt is only a necessary moment of a complex of conditions that are collectively sufficient for bringing about the given result. It is necessary only to the extent that the other conditions constituting the minimal sufficient conditions could not, in the absence of this condition, lead to the fire in the hall. However, by itself, it too might not have resulted in the same consequence. Had there been a fire alarm system or a sprinkler, the fire in the hall might have been averted.

The cause is here conceived of as an INUS condition, i.e., a condition that is an insufficient but necessary moment of a complex that is unnecessary but sufficient for producing the given effect. The lighted cigarette butt is insufficient by itself for producing the effect (fire) but it is a necessary moment of a complex of conditions $(XY\bar{Z})$, and the complex $XY\bar{Z}$ is collectively sufficient for the fire in the hall (effect) but it is not necessary because the same effect (fire in the hall) could have been caused by another complex (say, short circuiting, electric current in the wire and wooden panelling). Let us take another example: we might say that the mutiny in the naval ratings was the INUS condition for the transfer of power from the British to the Indians in August 1947. In other words, the mutiny was the necessary moment of a complex of conditions (say, popular participation in the Quit India movement, peasant uprisings, trade union movements and the presence of a Labour government in Britain) which was collectively sufficient for bringing about the transfer of power in 1947. However, this complex of conjunctive conditions was by no means necessary because another complex of conditions (e.g., adverse balance of payments, weakening of the imperial power after the war and new military obligations) could also have produced the same effect. Understood in this way, the essential difference between an INUS condition and a condition that is considered to be necessary under the circumstances is that the former (unlike the latter) refers to conjunctive conditions that enable the necessary moment to have the desired effect. Consequently, these conjunctive conditions are considered to be a part of the complex that constitutes the cause of that effect.

The notion of cause as an INUS condition takes into account the possibility of there being more than one complex of minimal sufficient conditions, and hence, it suggests that the condition C could be regarded as the cause (a necessary moment) only if it is a part of the complex of minimal sufficient conditions that was present at that time. However, if more than one complex of minimal sufficient conditions were present at the time of the occurrence of the event, it is assumed that C must be a condition that is common to both complexes of minimal sufficient conditions. There may of course be other minimal sufficient conditions that were not present at that time and C may not be a part of those complexes but that would not in any way undermine our conclusion that C is the cause of the particular effect. To put it in the language of philosophic discourse, one could say that C was a necessary and indispensable moment if: (i) only one minimal sufficient condition is present and C is a necessary moment of it; (ii) the condition C is a necessary moment of each of the minimal sufficient conditions present at that time; and (iii) C has the ability to combine with X, Y or

Z to produce the desired result.[30] Needless to say, the analysis rests upon our ability to identify a complex of minimal sufficient conditions that can bring about the given effect.

While speaking of cause as an INUS condition, it is important to mention that an INUS condition is specified in the context of a particular inquiry, i.e., it has an identified causal field. The lighted cigarette butt on the floor rather than the presence of oxygen in the air or the carpet on the floor is considered to be the cause of the fire in the hall because the other conditions are considered, in the context of this inquiry, to be 'permanent conditions' that are present under 'normal circumstances' when the fire did not occur. Consequently, the presence of the lighted cigarette butt is considered to be the moment that is a necessary and an indispensable part of the complex of conditions. Similarly, when we say that the mutiny in the naval ratings is the cause of the transfer of power, the causal field is the British raj in India and the Indian struggle for independence.[31]

The notion of an INUS condition approximates the social scientist's/historian's use of the term cause, hence it appears to be more adequate than the earlier conceptions of cause. However, it has at least one serious limitation which jeopardizes and questions its adequacy. It is difficult to apply this notion of cause to situations that are overdetermined, i.e., in situations where two or more minimal sufficient conditions containing different elements are present simultaneously, one cannot specify an INUS condition. For example, if our study of other instances of decolonization shows that the weakening of the imperial economy, new military obligations and the economic nonviability of continuing the administration of the colony constitute a complex of conditions that is collectively sufficient for decolonization, and our analysis of the Indian case reveals that these conditions existed along with another complex of minimal sufficient conditions (namely, a strong national movement for independence, peasant rebellions and a revolt in the army) which could also weaken the state

---

[30] For a detailed discussion of cause as an INUS condition, see J.L. Mackie, *The Cement of the Universe—A Study of Causation*, Oxford University Press, 1980, pp. 27–58.

[31] J.L. Mackie, 'Causes and Conditions', in E. Sosa, (ed.), 1975, pp. 34–6.

structure and consequently lead to decolonization, then under the circumstances, it would be difficult to specify a condition that was a necessary moment of a complex of conditions. Indeed, in instances of overdetermination it is exceedingly difficult to specify a necessary moment of any kind, that is, one cannot even specify a condition that was necessary contingently or under the circumstances. One could, in instances of multiple or independent overdetermination, ascertain the necessary moment by examining which of the possible sets of minimal sufficient conditions was present at the time. And even in instances of linked overdetermination, we could refer to the condition that was effective first as the moment that was necessary under the circumstances.[32] However, in situations of *simultaneous overdetermination*, it is difficult to undertake such an analysis. For example, if two bullets enter a man's heart simultaneously we cannot, even after the event, specify the bullet that was necessary for the effect (death of the individual). Similarly, if lightning strikes a barn in which a tramp had thrown a lighted cigarette on a stack of dry hay, then under the circumstances neither lightning nor the presence of the lighted cigarette could be regarded as a condition that was necessary for the result.[33] We cannot even say that each of them is a 'non-redundant part' of the complex condition because the barn would have burned down if either of the two conditions—lightning or the lighted cigarette—was present.

Let us take some other examples from the social sciences. If the rise in taxation by the ruling government coincides with the arrival of a

[32] In linked overdetermination, the situation is such that the two causal factors C and D are so linked that if the former is prevented from occurring it would trigger off a reaction that would lead to the occurrence of the latter. Since both C and D can produce the same effect, irrespective of the condition that is operative, the same result follows.

[33] These examples are used by K. Marc Wogau and M. Scriven respectively to point to the problems that are associated with identifying a necessary moment. Marc Wogau goes on to argue that every moment in the complex of minimal sufficient conditions must be seen as a necessary and a non-redundant part of the complex, but Scriven abandons the search for a necessary moment and defines cause as a moment that is contingently sufficient. See K.M. Wogau, 'On Historical Explanation', *Theoria*, vol. XXVIII, 1963, pt. III, pp. 222–4

new administrator at the local level—one whose style of functioning leads to frequent clashes with the local people—it would be exceedingly difficult to specify an INUS condition for the ensuing unrest. If we say that the minimal sufficient condition consists of both these conjuncts and that they are jointly sufficient for the effect, we cannot still specify the necessary moment in the INUS condition. Thus, as long as we acknowledge that any two of the conjunctive conditions present (at the time of the occurrence of the event) could by themselves or in association with other conditions bring about the given result, we cannot consider any of them individually as the moment that was necessary for the effect. So if we accept that both lightning and the lighted cigarette could have separately resulted in the burning down of the barn, we cannot say that either of them was a necessary moment of a complex that was sufficient but unnecessary for that effect. Similarly, if we recognize that rebellion in the ranks of the armed forces or the military and the strategic interests of the colonizer could in association with other conditions (such as the emergence of a national movement for independence, and the increasing economic burden of administering the colony) result in the transfer of power to the colonized, and we find that both these conditions were present at the time of the transfer of power to India in 1947, then neither of the two conditions can be considered as a necessary moment in the conjunctive complex because each is an insufficient and *unnecessary* moment of the complex that is perhaps unnecessary but sufficient for the effect. Thus, we would either have to abandon the notion of overdetermination and plurality of causes, or else, in instances of simultaneous overdetermination, accept that it is not possible for the social scientist to determine the necessary moment in the complex. Since the notion of necessity would be rendered superfluous if we were to argue that the entire set of conjunctive conditions is jointly necessary for the effect, by referring collectively to the conditions that preceded the event as the *cause*, we can only imply that the conjunction of conditions was *post hoc sufficient* for the given effect.

Recognizing this, some philosophers of social science argue that the term 'cause' denotes a condition that was 'contingently sufficient' for the effect, that is, it is a condition that need not be present for the event to occur, but, as it happens, in this instance it was present and it did, in the presence of other conditions, lead to the given effect. This conception of cause accepts that in the absence of C some other condition could have intervened and produced the same result; hence, it is not a condition that is essential and non-substitutible. All that we can say is that it was *contingently sufficient* for the given result because we know that the event occurred and we believe that the prevailing conditions must have been sufficient for the occurrence of that event. This would be particularly true of situations that are marked by simultaneous or linked overdetermination. In the case of the transfer of power where more than one of the conditions present could have produced the same result, the rebellion in the ranks of the armed forces, the military-strategic interests of the colonizer, or the economic burden of administering the colony can be designated as the condition that was necessary for the effect, yet, we can assert that each of them is contingently sufficient for the effect (transfer of power). In other words, while designating each of them as the cause of the transfer of power we might legitimately imply that each is a contingently sufficient condition.

The same notion of cause could be applied to instances of linked overdetermination. For example, in a situation where *A* and *B* are individually working to bring about the same effect (e.g., the fall of the ruling government) we may consider the actions of *A* (who is able to bring about a split in the members of the ruling party) as being contingently sufficient for the event because we know that had *A* not been successful in splitting the party, *B* would have done so, thereby producing the same result, namely, the fall of the government. It is sometimes argued that the actions of *A* may not appear to be necessary if the event being explained is regarded under the general description of 'toppling the government'. But if we are interested in explaining the precise nature of the event—the manner and the time of the event— then the actions of *A* would be both important and necessary for the explanation.[34] However, to consider the actions of *A* as being necessary for the effect, we would have to stipulate, under the circumstan-

---

[34] An argument of this kind is made by C. Behan McCullagh, *Justifying Historical Descriptions*, Cambridge University Press, Cambridge, 1984.

ces, that B would have acted at a slower pace than A and in a manner that was markedly different from that of A. In other words, we would require a series of counterfactual assertions about what might have happened in the absence of the actions of A: a task that is itself fraught with innumerable difficulties.[35]

Thus, even within the framework of singular causal assertions, the term 'cause' may be used to refer to a condition that is: (i) necessary under the circumstances, (ii) a necessary and non-redundant part of a minimal sufficient condition, (iii) an INUS condition, or (iv) a contingently sufficient condition. Although it is customary to refer to the cause as a condition that is necessary (at least retrospectively) for a given effect, this notion cannot easily be applied in the social sciences because most situations in the social world are overdetermined and, under those circumstances, it is exceedingly difficult to identify in the complex of conditions operating at that time, a moment that was necessary for an event. Besides, if we accept the claim that the precise nature of the event can be explained only by referring to the determinate conjunction of different conditions, then we can consider only the set of conditions prevailing at that time to be collectively responsible and indispensable for the effect. If we maintain that each of the conditions present is a necessary and a non-redundant moment, then it is the responsibility of the social scientist to show that the absence of any of these conditions would have made a substantial difference to the nature of the event; further, that the replacement of any one condition, say C_2 by C_6, would not have neutralized that effect, and the absence of C_2 would not itself have led to the emergence of C_8 that would have produced the same effect. Besides, the use of the notion of necessity in this manner would only make it a formal and empty concept. For these reasons, while explaining historical events it is often preferable to invoke only the relationship of sufficiency and assert that conditions $C_1 \ldots C_n$ were *sufficient* to bring about the given effect, that is, their collective or individual presence ensures the consequence.

The relationship of sufficiency can be, and often is, established by

---

[35] For a discussion of the logic of counterfactuals and the construction of 'possible worlds', see J. Elster, *Logic and Society*, John Wiley & Sons, Chichester, 1978, pp. 181–92.

using techniques of causal analysis or else by referring to historical counterexamples. In the case of the latter the investigator may argue that the cause specified is a condition that is sufficient/contingently sufficient either because all the other conditions existed over a period of time without producing that effect, or that similar conditions in comparable situations did not generate the same result. Expressing the same thing somewhat differently, the historian may argue that the causal explanations he opposes are insufficient on the ground that they identify a condition that was present at an earlier date and that it did not, despite the existence of reasonably similar conditions, produce the given result. For instance, they may argue that the epidemic was an insufficient condition for the decimation of the population because the same area had experienced severe epidemics in the earlier half of the century, which had not however produced the same result. Or else, using documentary evidence they may show that the conditions referred to by other historians in their explanation of that event did not actually exist: records reveal that some other conditions were present instead. For example, disputing the claim that the Rajput war was partly the result of Aurangzeb's policy of discrimination against the Rajputs, the historian may argue that the majority of the Rajput *mansabdars* were not alienated, and that Aurangzeb did not tolerate or encourage any well-marked factions and groupings. Further, that factions and groups emerged only in the last days of his rule.

What is perhaps important to note is that the relationship of sufficiency is established in a manner that is not significantly different from the way the relationship of necessity is established even within the positivist framework. Both refer to counterexamples and contrast cases to justify their claims. However, there is one important difference between the two. On the basis of a condition that is necessary for the effect we can hope to control our environment; by introducing or eliminating that condition under similar circumstances, we can ensure the occurrence or non-occurrence of that event. However, we cannot, even theoretically, make that claim on the basis of a sufficient condition. In other words, we cannot assert that the absence of C_1 would imply the absence of E. All that we can say is that in the presence of other conditions, C_1 was sufficient for E. We do not claim that the absence of this condition would imply the non-occurrence of the given event. Consequently, causal explanations of this kind (that refer to a contingently sufficient condition) cannot serve a technical interest.

It is indeed paradoxical that the notion of cause that is most appropriate for the social sciences is one that undermines the very ground on which causal explanations are frequently privileged and justified. By dissociating explanation from prediction and relinquishing the search for general laws, it renders these explanations incapable of serving the technical interest. Consequently, one is impelled to look beyond causal explanations and explore other ways of explaining an occurrence. There are three other considerations that lead us in the same direction. First, the conception of cause as a contingently sufficient condition accepts that 'there are virtually no known sufficient conditions, since human or accidental interference is almost inexhaustibly present . . . ',[36] yet, there is no place in its explanatory design for the actions of individuals. Second, in all its different forms, the causal explanation addresses the question:'Why did X happen?' or 'What C caused/will cause E?'. It regards other associated questions such as, 'How did X happen?' as supplements of the causal question that can be translated into causal questions of the 'What caused' kind.[37] Hence, it de-emphasizes questions about 'who', 'what', 'when',

[36] M. Scriven, 1964, p. 409.

[37] While answering questions like (i) 'How did the fire occur?' (ii) 'How did the Roman empire decline?' we can say:

  (i) When the gas leaking from the cylinder X came into contact with a nearby flame, the building was set ablaze.
  (ii) The centre could not control the far-flung regions of the empire. Internal dissensions grew and these regions were easily conquered by the neighbouring power, thereby weakening the empire.

Even though these questions and responses are not of the causal form, nevertheless, they can easily be translated into a causal interrogative. For example, we can say:

  (i) What caused the gas leak to result in the fire?
  (ii) What caused some of the regions to break from the empire?

Correspondingly, we can transform the answer and reply:

  (i) Allowing the leaked gas to come into contact with the flame caused the fire.
  (ii) Distance and diminishing control of the centre over these regions led to their breaking away and/or being conquered by the neighbouring powers.

and 'where'. Historians particularly argue that it is these questions that
need to be emphasized. Answering 'what happened' is as important
as answering 'why' something happened.[38] Consequently, we need a
mode of inquiry that is sensitive to questions of this kind. Third,
situations, actions and outcomes analysed by the social scientist are
not mere happenings or events; they are structures with meaning. To
explain what happened and why it happened the social scientist must
focus on the dimension of meaning: meaning that a particular action
had for those agents and the manner in which it was perceived and
understood by others. Reference to the dimension of meaning is necessary both for recognizing the distinctive nature of the object that the
social scientist analyses and to comprehend the specific attributes of a
particular social formation. In so far as the causal form of explanation
does not accommodate questions of this sort within its explanatory
design one has to seriously consider other modes of explaining and
understanding social phenomena.

[38] W. Dray, for instance, argues that the historian does not only try to explain
why the revolution occurred, he also examines whether the revolution was a
bourgeois revolution or a movement for national liberation. Analysing *what
happened* is an integral part of his inquiry and it cannot be subsumed under the
'why' interrogative. See W. Dray, *Laws and Explanation in History*, Clarendon Press,
Oxford, 1970, pp. 156–69.

II

Reason-Action Explanation

While causal explanations explain an historical event by referring to those conditions whose presence made the crucial difference to the outcome, reason-action explanations examine the actions of historical agents and explain why they choose to act in a particular way by identifying the reasons for their actions. The advocates of reason-action explanation assert that historical occurrences are not just events or happenings. They are performances: the doings of determinate historical agents. Explaining them in terms of what happened to men or what they undergo is, therefore, inadequate. We need to analyse instead what men do and why they do what they do.

Implicit in this form of argument is the belief that the nature of the object of inquiry in the social sciences is quite different from that in the natural sciences, and this difference necessitates the use of an alternative mode of explanation. Objects analysed in the natural sciences have an objective existence independent of the investigator; they are governed by laws that also operate independently of that investigator. Since the laws that govern the functioning of natural reality cannot be altered by the natural scientist, he can only manipulate and increase his control over nature by altering the conditions in which these laws operate. The social scientist, on the other hand, deals with objects that are constituted by men and occurrences in the social world that are the direct or indirect consequences of the actions of men. Hence, the object in the social sciences cannot be treated merely as a happening in the objective world; it must be conceived of as a performance. Modes of explanation, such as causal explanations, that see these performances as events are, for this reason, inadequate. Two kinds of arguments are used to support the need for a mode of explanation other than the causal. First, the nature of the object requires the use of explanations of the reason-action kind. Second, significant historical events—for example, revolts, rebellions, declarations of war and peace, treaties, campaigns, policy declarations, etc.—are all 'doings'. They are performances of groups and individuals. Although what happens in each instance cannot be reduced to the actions of any one individual or group, nevertheless, it cannot be explained or understood without reference to the actions of the agents.

Actions are, in this framework, distinguished from events or happenings. They are seen as performances that are intended and purposeful.[1] While they involve bodily movements and observable happenings they are not reducible to a sequence of movements and events. In fact, the same set of movements may represent different actions and the same action may involve different movements. For example, the closing and opening of the upper eyelid may constitute winking or blinking, and by raising my arm, I may be signalling to my friend or voting in the assembly. Similarly, the act of voting may involve different observable movements, such as the raising of the arm or the stamping of the ballot paper. Consequently, what differentiates a sequence of movements from an action is the reference to intentionality and what distinguishes one action from another is the intention of the agent. For instance, it is the intention of the agent that differentiates winking from blinking and the act of greeting from the attempt to get recognition from the chair to take the floor of the house. Hence, explanation of an action, unlike that of an event, requires a reference to the intentions, motives and beliefs of the individual. We can describe the act of voting by referring to a series of movements—

---

[1] This must not however be taken to imply that all actions are deliberate and involve conscious decisions by agents. Actors may sometimes follow habits or perform roles, and to explain such actions we would need a different kind of explanation. But in so far as actors sometimes do things that are the consequence of deliberation and conscious decision, we need to ask what prompted them to act in this manner.

for example, picking up the ballot paper, holding of the ink marker, stamping on an empty space against the name and symbol of a particular candidate, etc.,—but reference to these movements would not by itself constitute an action. As purposeful and intended behaviour, an action has a certain meaning in the context in which it is performed, and this meaning, it is argued, can be recovered by referring to the intentions and reasons for an action. Consequently, it is to the latter that we must turn in order to understand and make sense of an action.

By excluding the dimension of intentionality, causal explanations visualize history as a series of events. They examine what happens to men rather than what they do. In other words, they do not pause to consider why particular agents choose to act in a particular way. Reason-action explanations, on the other hand, assume that historical agents are rational men; they choose a particular course of action because they feel, on the basis of their assessment of the situation, that it would enable them to pursue and realize their goals, desires and interests. Hence, by referring to these goals, desires and intentions we can identify the *reasons* for the choices they make and the actions they embark upon. For instance, we can explain A's decision to go on a diet by referring to his intention to lose weight. Similarly, we can explain B's decision to join the army by pointing to his intense patriotic desire to serve the country.

Intentions and actions are not always, however, linked in this simple and direct manner. Sometimes intentions are not translated into actions and, on other occasions, they may be translated into different actions. For example, two people may have the same desire and intention to lose weight but they may not both decide to go on a diet. The difference in their action may arise on two grounds: first, A may believe that changing his diet and checking the calorie intake is the best way to lose weight but B may, with good reason, believe that exercise is the best way to lose weight. Hence, depending upon their assessment of the different means for the realization of their intention, they may perform different actions. Second, on comparing different desires and coexisting wants, they may decide not to pursue a particular desire and intention. B may have the intention of losing weight; he may also believe that dieting is the best way to lose weight, but he may continue to eat the high calorie food available in the University cafeteria instead of going to another restaurant in town because he does not want to waste his time commuting the distance when his final exams are only a month away. Hence, on the basis of a comparative assessment of his different wants (losing weight and getting a first in the exams) he may decide not to act upon a particular intention.[2] Let us take another example: C may want to contest elections because he is interested in being elected to the parliament. However, he knows that if he is elected to the parliament he will have little time to pursue his interest in genetic engineering. Consequently, on appraising his different wants, he may decide not to stand for elections; that is, he may act in a manner that would not enable him to realize his desire to be a member of parliament. Thus, one finds that all desires and intentions do not always get translated into action and even the same intentions do not lead to the performance of the same action.

However, as and when intentions are translated into action, they are accompanied by the belief that acting in the chosen way will yield the desired result, i.e., it will enable the agent to realize his goals, desires and wants. This belief may be wrong or mistaken; it may be based on insufficient information or an inaccurate assessment of different alternatives, yet it is the presence of this belief that prompts the agent to act in that particular way and it is this that furnishes him with the rationale for his action.[3] A's intention to lose weight expresses itself in his decision to change his diet and reduce his calorie intake when it is accompanied by the belief that this is the best possible way or the best available means for the realization of that intention. Similarly, X's desire to contest elections for the parliament furnishes him with a reason to join party P_2 only when it is associated with the belief that

[2] We are, of course, assuming that A and B are placed in similar circumstances because the difference in their circumstances may otherwise result in their performing the same action even when they hold different beliefs. B may not, for instance, believe in absolute terms that exercise is the best way to lose weight. However, given the absence of health food restaurants, he may decide that it is the best possible way of losing weight. So the difference in the action may be related to the differences in the circumstances in which each of them is placed.

[3] See D. Milligan, *Reasoning and the Explanation of Action*, Humanities Press Inc., New Jersey, 1980, pp. 105–14; and P. Achinstein, *The Nature of Explanation*, Oxford University Press, New York, 1983, pp. 164–6.

party P_1 will not offer him a party ticket from that constituency. Hence, one needs to refer both to the intention and the accompanying belief and for the latter, one needs to analyse the agent's perception of his situation and the actions of other agents. In other words, one must see how the agent assessed the situation and weighed the alternative courses of action available to him at that time. This is the minimal requirement of a reason-action explanation.

Most advocates of reason-action explanation maintain that the reasons identified must be those that were avowed by the agents themselves. Reference to the agent's avowed reason is considered to be necessary because they feel that there is no other way of determining whether the reason adduced in the explanation is actually *the* reason for the agent's chosen action.[4] For instance, on seeing *A* light a fire in his living room on a cold winter evening we may infer that he is expecting a visitor and he is lighting the fire to keep the room warm. In other words, we may conclude on the basis of our observation of his daily practices and acceptable behaviour, that the expected visit is his reason for lighting the fire and sitting in this room. Without reference to his avowed reasons we have no way of knowing that his reason for the action may be quite different. To identify his reasons correctly and to know that he is sitting there, perhaps to finish the book he is reading because this room is better lighted than the others, one needs to refer to his statements and avowed reasons.

However, explanations of an agent's action in terms of his avowed reasons present at least four problems. First, agents do not always give reasons for their actions, so it is not always possible to refer to avowed reasons. Second, even when they do give reasons there is no way of determining that the avowed reason is the 'real' reason for performing that action. Third, most often historical agents give reasons retrospectively to justify their action and to make it appear reasonable. Fourth, while explaining the same action historical agents sometimes offer

---

[4] See N.S. Sutherland, 'Motives as Explanations', *Mind*, vol. LXVIII, no. 70, April 1959, pp. 145–59; D. Davidson, 'Actions, Reasons and Causes', *Journal of Philosophy*, vol. LX, no. 23, 1963, pp. 685–700; D. Bennet, 'Action, Reason, and Purpose', *Journal of Philosophy*, vol. LXII, no. 4, 1965, pp. 85–96; J.E. White, 'Avowed Reasons and Causal Explanation', *Mind*, vol. LXXX, New Series, no. 80, 1971, pp. 238–45.

different reasons to different audiences. Consequently, we have to choose between different avowals and there is no a priori criterion for privileging one assertion over another. For instance, while explaining the decision of the British to transfer power to India in 1947, we may consider the reasons given by the British Government in India in its cabinet meetings as being more reliable and authentic than those that are avowed before the British Parliament on the ground that the Labour government would have faced serious criticism from the members of the Conservative party if they had publicly claimed that Britain could not, under the prevailing circumstances, administer the colony. In this instance we might decide that giving greater importance to the reasons avowed in cabinet meetings would be appropriate, but it is possible to conceive of other situations where the public assertions might be more significant for determining the reasons for an action. At the party meeting a minister may explain his resignation from the cabinet of ministers on the ground that the party has been neglecting the problems of his constituency but he may tell the press that he is resigning to protest against the party's new policy on education. In this case, the public assertions would be as, if not more, important than the reason given to his colleagues in a closed door meeting. And if his resignation coincides with the announcement of fresh elections and the resignation of other party members, then both these avowed reasons may appear insufficient. One might, in those circumstances, refer to the anticipated consequences of such an action before the elections—such as, a stronger bargaining position—as a possible reason for the action even though it is not avowed by the agent at any time.

Social scientists often set aside reasons avowed by the agent on the ground that that they are nonverifiable.[5] Since they may be feigned

---

[5] According to White, 'My avowed reasons may be insincere, feigned or genuine but it does not make sense to say that they are "mistaken" in the same sense as statements like "It is raining" can be mistaken. It is possible to prove that the statement, "It is raining in Denver", is mistaken. But it is impossible to prove one mistaken in the same way when I honestly say, "I hurt" '. In other words, such assertions are not subject to the same criterion of empirical verification, and it is for this attribute that social scientists reject this mode of analysis. J.E. White, ibid., p. 244.

or avowed *post hoc* to provide a justification for the act, they cannot, according to its critics, provide an adequate basis for explaining an action. For example, on noticing that the support for the strike is gradually diminishing, the student leaders may decide to call off the strike, but to justify their action to their supporters they may assert that the continuation of the strike may lead to the closure of the university, and, to prevent the administration from taking such a decision, they are withdrawing the strike. It is equally possible that the agent may be unaware of or even mistaken about his reasons. *A* may, for instance, donate to different charities because he thinks that he must help the needy but he may be unaware of the fact that he is trying to impress others and gain recognition by this action.

Given these difficulties, historians frequently set aside avowed reasons and try to specify the reason for an action through an analysis of the existing situation and the expressed intentions of the agent. In other words, by referring to the existing situation they try to determine what would have been the appropriate and rational action for the agent, and vice versa, given the performance of an action by the agent, they would try to show that the action was rational and it made 'perfectly good sense' from the agent's point of view: i.e., in the context of his intentions, an assessment of the situation and the actions of others, the chosen action was the thing to do.[6] Reason-action explanations of this kind or rational explanations as they are sometimes called,[7] rest on the assumption that certain kinds of actions make perfectly good sense in certain situations, particularly in the presence of certain intentions and motives. They suggest that certain kinds of intentions accord easily with certain kinds of actions. While it is not necessary that a particular intention will result in the performance of an action, nevertheless, the possibility of certain actions being per-

[6] See R.S. Peters, J. McCraken and J.O. Urmson, 'Symposium: Motives and Causes', *Proceedings of the Aristotelian Society*, Supplementary, vol. XXVI, 1952, pp. 139–94.

[7] See R.F. Atkinson, *Knowledge and Explanation in History*, Macmillan, London, 1978, pp. 115–28; W. Dray, 'The Historical Explanation of Action Reconsidered', B. Mazlish, 'Rational Explanations in History', and Kai Nielsen, 'Rational Explanations in History', in S. Hook (ed.), *Philosophy and History: A Symposium*, New York University Press, New York, 1963, pp. 105–35, 275–85, 296–324.

formed remains; and, if any of those actions are performed they make 'perfectly good sense' and require no further explanation. For example, we may not be able to say that all leaders withdraw or will withdraw a movement if it is losing support. Nevertheless, if the movement is withdrawn, and if the withdrawal was preceded by reports of the movement losing momentum, then it appears quite reasonable and rational to accept that the latter provided sufficient reason for the decision to withdraw the movement. Consequently, by linking the assessment of the situation with the agent's motives and beliefs they explain an agent's decision to act in a particular way.

Reason-action explanations assume that historical agents are rational beings: they have reasons and grounds for making a particular choice and acting in a particular way. Consequently, the task of the investigator is to identify the considerations that must have weighed in the agent's deliberations. These considerations could be several. They may relate to his assessment of the possibilities open to him in that situation, the anticipated actions of other agents, the implications and consequences of the action, and the relative cost of pursuing that course of action. Accordingly, while explaining the action of an agent, the historian must take cognizance of each of these considerations. Since the considerations that would weigh with any agent can be known from an understanding of ourselves and from the study of other comparable cases, it is assumed that we can, on the basis of our experience and previous study, delineate the possible considerations that would appear important to any agent.

Rational explanations of this kind are, it is argued, offered by men in the course of everyday life. On seeing a student gathering litter from the school corridor after school hours, we infer that the student has been made to stay back and do this job as punishment for something that he might have done earlier in the day. Consequently, to understand the action of the teacher we try to find out what the student had done that warranted punishment. When we find out that the student had not attended the maths class and that the maths teacher had given detention to the student, we conclude that abstention from class was the reason for the punishment of the student. In reaching this conclusion we assume that the student's behaviour warranted this action; that is, it was reasonable for a teacher to punish a student who stayed away from class. It is reasonable because we can expect other teachers to take similar action under similar circumstances.[8]

While making inferences of this kind, we assume that there are certain normal or acceptable ways of responding to a particular predicament. Consequently, by referring to the way the situation appeared to the agent and invoking the code of normal/expected behaviour, we endeavour to explain and make sense of the agent's action.[9] Thus, by arguing that the student's absence from class was seen by the agent (teacher) as wilful neglect of work and improper conduct, and believing (like most other people) that such behaviour must not be tolerated or encouraged, the teacher decided to punish the student by asking her to stay back after school and help the janitor to clean up the corridors and the blackboards. It is, of course, entirely possible that the agent might have been misinformed or that she could have misunderstood the behaviour of the student. For instance, the maths teacher could be mistaken in thinking that the student deliberately and wilfully stayed away from class; it is possible that she had been asked by another teacher to help with the preparations for the annual day celebrations. Nevertheless, to explain the action it is sufficient to see how the situation was perceived by the agent and what was, under those circumstances, the thing to do.

Reference to the antecedent situation is necessary for identifying the reason for an action, and historians who use this mode of explanation make considerable effort to present a picture of the then existing situation and to show that the constructed picture was either shared by the agent or available to him; hence, it could provide the basis for his taking the decision he did. However, it is important at this juncture to mention that a reference to the antecedent condition is not always

---

[8] Teachers may vary the nature of punishment, but they would agree that the action of the student warranted some sort of punishment.

[9] This conception is grounded philosophically in the Weberian belief that actions manifest purposes and certain kinds of actions follow logically from certain kinds of motives. Consequently, it encourages the formation of ideal constructs that relate particular types of actions to corresponding motives. For a detailed discussion, see A. Schutz, 'Concept and Theory Formation in the Social Sciences', in M. Natanson (ed.), *Philosophy of the Social Sciences: A Reader*, Random House, New York, 1963, pp. 231–49.

sufficient for explaining the choice of a determinate action. For the latter one needs to supplement the agent's assessment of the situation with an analysis of his pattern of beliefs. To explain the decision to withdraw the agitation it is not sufficient to say that the movement was losing momentum; one needs also to show that the agent (leader, in this instance) believed that if the movement fizzled out it would fail to serve the purpose for which it was launched. To put it somewhat differently, one would have to argue that the movement was launched primarily to put pressure on the administration to enter into negotiations, hence it could be withdrawn before the avowed objective had been accomplished. In fact, on seeing that it was losing ground support, it would be imperative to withdraw the movement as and when the appropriate opportunity arose because that would enable the agitating party to show its strength and enter negotiations from a position of strength.

To identify the reason in this way by analysing the agent's assessment of the situation requires a degree of empirical research. For example, to determine the reason for A's decision to eat at salad bars rather than at MacDonalds we may, on the basis of previous study and knowledge of human behaviour, suggest that there could be four possible reasons for this decision by an individual: (i) Salad bars are less crowded at lunch time; (ii) A wanted to lose weight; (iii) a change of diet was recommended by the doctor on medical grounds; (iv) meat used in the burger chains like MacDonalds is responsible for the destruction of the rain forests. To determine which of these considerations weighed in the case of A, we would need to analyse the situation in which the agent lived. We would need to see if A was frequenting salad bars only at lunch time and whether the salad bars were less crowded than MacDonalds at that hour. If our study reveals that most of the residents in that colony eat at salad bars then we cannot assert that A eats at the salad bar because it is less crowded at lunch time. One might then have to consider the possibility of A going there to join a friend who eats or perhaps works at the salad bar. Similarly, one would have to determine whether A visited his doctor in the recent past who could have recommended the change of diet, or if A has a medical problem that warrants this decision. We might even see if A supports environmentalist and other ecological groups that work for the preservation of the earth's environment. If A is known to avoid those things that lead to the destruction of or imbalance in the ecological system we may accept that (iv) is the reason for his action. We would be justified in reaching this conclusion because it coheres with his previous actions and it follows logically from his ideological commitments and beliefs. Similarly, to explain the actions of a president who has approved the expenditure in military affairs while cutting all other estimated budgetary demands, we might on the basis of other studies and a conception of rational behaviour, suggest that a president would not cut military expenditure under the following conditions: (i) he needs the support of the military to remain in power, so he has to accept their demands; (ii) he fears an aggression from the neighbouring country; (iii) the country needs to modernize the army. If the survey of relevant data shows that the state personnel did not feel that any neighbouring country would attack them at that time, and we also find that the military personnel possess equipment that is more advanced than that of his neighbours, it seems reasonable to conclude that neither (ii) nor (iii) could be considered as possible reasons for the president's action. One would then have to see if (i) is applicable or whether the situation warrants a search for other possible reasons. From the point of view of reason-action explanations it is important for the historian to analyse how the agent perceived the situation rather than what was in actuality the case.[10] In this case, it would be important to see if the president or the associated personnel believed that the neighbouring country might attack them and not if the neighbouring country was actually in a position to attack them. It is possible that official documents have revealed to the historian the unpreparedness of the neighbouring country such that it seems highly improbable that it would attack another, but if this information was not available to the other government or if the official records of the latter do not show any awareness of this, then the historian is justified in arguing that the threat of war was the reason for the president's decision to approve military expenditure.

One need only reiterate that in all such instances, it is assumed that

[10] See W. Dray, *Laws and Explanation in History*, Clarendon Press, Oxford, 1970, pp. 125-6.

any rational agent or at least one performing the same role and function as *A* would have acted in a similar manner. And the particular response seems to us to be warranted or appropriate only to that extent. To return to the case of the punished student, we consider absence from class to be the reason for the punishment because we accept that neglect of work and rude behaviour warrant punishment. If absence from class was not seen as a sign of improper conduct, we would look for other reasons for the action. Thus, while providing reasons for an action the analyst frequently draws upon his experience and understanding of himself and others, and in the process he assumes, at least implicitly, that the knower and the known (the agent and the analyst) are similar. Consequently, considerations that would weigh with one would also weigh with the other and what appears to one as the rational thing to do would also make sense to the other. This belief that is central to most reason-action explanation is beset with a number of difficulties. Presupposing the transferability of agents it ignores that what is an accepted and reasonable thing to do is often culture-bound; it is at least institution- and society-specific. In our society it may be the done thing to give detention to students for wilful neglect of work but this may not be the acceptable thing in another society; indeed, punishing young students may itself be an idea that is culture-specific. Besides, staying back after school may appear, given the norms in which I have been socialized, as a form of detention. In another institution, it may be the expected duty and responsibility of students of class IX and X to take turns to stay back and help the janitor clean the place. Hence, to eliminate the possibility of error in identifying the agent's reason for an action, we need to refer to the accepted pattern and norms of behaviour of that agent; minimally, one needs to refer to and be acquainted with the institution- and group-specific attributes while identifying the reasons for an agent's behaviour. For example, to specify the reasons for the decision of the student community to go on strike it would not be sufficient to refer to the preceding or antecedent situation. If the strike is preceded by an increase in the hostel fee, it might appear that the students went on strike to protest against this decision of the authorities. However, if the call for the strike is given in August, just before the annual student union elections, and we find that a call for strike is frequently given by the student leadership at that period in time, one would also need to take into account the electoral considerations while stipulating the reasons for the action of the union leadership. In other words, one would have to take into account at least the peculiarities of institutional behaviour and practices while determining what is the norm of accepted behaviour for the agent. Let us consider another possibility. If the call for strike given in August (a time when previous unions have looked for an opportunity to launch a student protest) is preceded by hostel problems (e.g., a large number of students have been denied hostel accommodation) then, on the basis of the criterion just outlined, it would be difficult to determine the reason for the agent's action. Similarly, if the student punished by the teacher is a girl guide who also wishes to be nominated the school captain, then it is possible that her action may have been motivated by either of these desires. In fact, one would have to consider both these motivations while identifying the reason for her action. One could, of course, rely on the agent's avowed reasons or her assertions (a strategy that is frequently used by historians) but reliance on avowed reasons is, as we argued earlier, quite problematic. Consequently, one would need to take into account the student's behaviour on previous occasions, her pattern of beliefs and values to see if either or both of these considerations were the reason for the action of the agent. In other words, one would have to construct a picture of the agent—his beliefs, values, pattern of behaviour, professed strategy—in order to determine, with any degree of accuracy and reliability, the agent's reason for an action.

One needs to refer to the agent's pattern of beliefs and values for another reason also. While identifying the agent's reason for an action we assume that the agent would choose a course of action that appears to be the most rational thing to do under the circumstances, given his assessment of the situation. However, this assumption is not always warranted. In some instances, the agents may not choose the most rational course of action; they may instead decide to act in a manner that conforms to their previous behaviour or accords with other ideals that they consider to be valuable. For example, the decision to dissociate oneself from a party which most people think is going to perform badly in the forthcoming elections may appear to be the rational thing to do if a person wants to win elections. Yet, we may find that an agent A may not actually take this decision. He may, despite his desire to win elections, stay with his party. Under these circumstances, one would have to explain why the agent acted in this way even though, given his assessment of the situation and his own intentions, this does not appear to be the rational thing to do. In such situations one would need to analyse the agent's behaviour on previous occasions, refer to his other beliefs and values to determine the reason for the action.[11] In other words, it is only by constructing a picture of the agent—his beliefs, values, intentions, preferred strategy, etc.,— that we can determine whether the inferred reasons are or could be the agent's reasons for the action.[12]

While accounts of this kind seek to identify what might, in all probability, be the reason for the action of the agent, they assume and often postulate a high degree of consistency and coherence in the actions of the individual. While explaining the actions of leaders and groups it looks for the professed objectives, goals and strategies for action and analyses a particular action as an instance of the identified objectives, plans and strategies: it sees each action as the working-out of the stipulated goals and strategies. Apart from debating the adequacy of the goals, beliefs and principles invoked, one also needs to question whether particular decisions can be adequately explained in terms of the stipulated strategies. A leader's assertion that the time was just right for launching the agitation may, at one level, provide the reason for the agent's action. However, it might be difficult to explain this decision and judgment about the timing of the movement with reference to the identified strategy. In other words, it might be difficult to justify the decision on the ground that this was, given the assess-

[11] One is here referring only to that which is a minimal requirement for determining the reason for an action. The actual identification of a reason from among the several possibilities is undoubtedly a more complex process. It involves an analysis of the agent's objectives, goals, plans, strategy, beliefs and values in order to delineate the possible reasons for the agent's action, and since none of these are simply given to the historian they have to be constructed by him from the available records.

[12] The task of constructing a picture of the agent, ideally with reference to his world-view, is a difficult and complex one and must rely on the hermeneutic skills of systematic exegesis, and it is the absence of the latter that is frequently responsible for the inadequacy of the reason-action explanation.

ment of the situation, the thing to do. While it is generally quite legitimate to assume that significant historical actions, unlike everyday behaviour, are the consequence of careful deliberation, nevertheless, a whole range of decisions, such as the timing of the movement and the anticipated responses of the other actors, rely on an intuitive grasp of the mood of the people. To argue retrospectively that this was the rational thing to do or that it was a logical consequence of the accepted strategy seems a little misplaced.

There is another attribute of reason-action explanations that needs to be considered in some detail. Since the purpose of such explanations is to show that the deed/action performed was the 'thing to do' from the agent's point of view, it is often argued that such explanations tend to be justificatory in nature. They do not ask if the agent's decision or his assessment of the situation was correct or valid. Making a distinction between the historical experience and the lived experience of the agent, the advocates of such explanations maintain that the question of the correctness of an action must not be asked for the following reasons: (i) The appropriateness of an action or the decision can be judged only retrospectively and with reference to the actual outcome of the interplay of various conditions. (ii) Since the outcome (the historical event) is the result of a variety of contending forces which are not within the control of any agent, action must not be judged in terms of its consequences. It must instead be analysed with reference to the agent's intentions and motives. (iii) There is a difference between the writing of history and the making of history. Knowing what happened, the historian can easily determine whether a particular course of action chosen by the agent was appropriate or not. Besides, with the material available to him the historian is better informed about the intentions and plans of other agents and the happenings in different places of which the agent may not have been aware. In other words, the agent chooses a particular course of action that seems appropriate to him given his world-view and the limitations of the information available to him. He has no way of knowing, in advance, the consequence of his action and that of others'. The historian knows what did happen and the difference in their world-view and this information make a crucial difference in determining the correctness of an action. (iv) Retrospectively, one can draw lessons from the so-called failures and successes of the plans and actions of different groups and individuals: indeed, on seeing what happened, the agents occasionally realize that their decisions were wrong—they were based on an incorrect assessment of the situation and the actions of others or on insufficient information. Nevertheless, it would be quite erroneous to judge the correctness of the action on that basis. (v) From the point of historical investigation it is more important to ask why the agents embarked on a particular course of action and to explain why they did what they did. The question of what they ought to have done is, historically speaking, less warranted. The task of the historian is to explain what happened and not to apportion blame and praise among different agents. Besides, one can, in the manner of a juror, pin the moral responsibility of the performance of an action on some agent but it is extremely difficult to hold an agent responsible for the historical event. Consequently, it is far more important to explain why the agent acted in a particular way, that is, to uncover his beliefs—even if they were wrong or mistaken—that prompted him to choose that action. It is for these various reasons that reason-action explanations focus on the agent and try and explain his decisions and choices from his perspective.

On the strength of these arguments one is inclined to accept the claim that the historian should explain the action of an agent by referring to his own reasons (avowed or inferred). However, the problem with reason-action explanations is that they are unable to perform just this task. They assume that the knower and the known, the historian and the agent, are essentially similar. Consequently, expectations of behaviour that appear normal and warranted to one must appear similarly to the other. In making this assumption it ignores the distinctiveness of the world-views, values and beliefs of different agents. To put it differently, it brackets the historicality of agents and assumes that human nature is the same and that there are certain known and given patterns of intention-action interrelationship. To recover the agent's reasons for an action it is essential to employ hermeneutic skills of exegesis to reconstruct the agent's life world. It is only through the mode of hermeneutic understanding that we can make sense of the assertions and expressions of an historical agent and assert that the reason identified could be a reason even for the agent and that the reason inferred from the avowals of the agent did actually constitute a reason for those historically specific agents. Implicit here is the assumption that what we consider to be the reason for that category of actions, and vice versa what was for them a reason may not be ignored because it does not appear to us to be a reason that warrants the given action.

Critics argue that what happened in history cannot be reduced to or understood merely in terms of the actions of any one individual or group in society. Further, that human actions cannot be studied by themselves, isolated from everything else, because they are circumscribed by conditions that are not entirely under the control of any individual. Material and ideological structures constrain human actions; they impinge on the choice of a particular course of action as well as its outcome. Men, we find, participate in history with different intentions but what happens is something that no one had perhaps intended. Consequently, what happened in history cannot be reduced to the intentions of agents, and events cannot be understood merely as the products of human action. A reference to the context of objective structures in which men live and participate in social and political life must form a necessary part of an historical explanation. For this reason they feel that reason-action explanations serve a limited purpose; while they can help us to explain the actions of the agent they are unable to explain the occurrence of the historical event.

Although we have, in our discussion, referred primarily to the actions of individual actors, the same pattern of explanation is frequently used by historians to account for the actions of groups and other collectivities, such as political parties, trade unions, capitalist enterprises, armies, political and educational institutions, etc. Referring to the latter as social actors,[13] they argue that these actors also have a means of formulating and reaching decisions. Like individuals, they pursue their desires and deliberate upon the different ways of realizing those desires. Consequently, their actions reflect the same considerations as those of determinate individuals. While most of these theorists make a distinction between individual and social actors

---

[13] Barry Hindess, 'Analyzing Actors' Choices', *American Political Science Review*, vol. 11, 1990, no. 1, pp. 87–97.

and maintain that the latter cannot be reduced to the former, nevertheless, in their analysis of the actions, desires and goals of these social actors they stress the identity in the perception of these collective bodies. To explain the determinate decisions and choices of the group they invariably turn to the recorded assertions of a few individuals, mostly leaders and other eminent personalities within that group. As a result their explanation of the actions of the collective entity frequently suffers from an elitist bias and reflects many of the errors associated with methodological individualism.

Before concluding our discussion on reason-action explanations, it is necessary to reflect on a claim that we have merely presupposed in our discussion, namely, that reason-action explanations form a separate form of explanation, quite distinct from causal explanations. This assumption needs to be examined carefully because it has been challenged by several theorists who argue that the structure of a reason-action explanation is similar to that of the covering law model. According to them, when we explain an action by referring to a reason or disposition, we presuppose the existence of a general law on the basis of which we link that intention/disposition to a particular behaviour.[14] For example, to argue that abstention from class was the reason for the punishment of the student by the teacher we presuppose the existence of a law which suggests that students are punished by their teachers for wilfully neglecting their work. To put it somewhat differently, when we explain the action of the teacher, we make an argument of the following kind: T (teacher) was in a situation characterized by condition C (absence of a student from class); when anyone is in a situation of the C kind, the thing to do is A (give punishment); therefore, T did A.[15]

---

[14] When we explain an action by linking it to a motive we assume a law-like generalization of the sort: 'Under conditions $C_1 \ldots C_n$ men who desire X act in the manner $A_1 \ldots A_n$. Similarly, while explaining in terms of dispositions we assume that 'When conditions $C_1 \ldots C_n$ prevail, anything with A manifests B'. Thus, when we say that a person acted from a certain motive we subsume his behaviour under a general law of the causal kind and consider his behaviour as an instance of the typical kind. Carl G. Hempel, 'Reasons and Covering Laws in Historical Explanations', in S. Hook (ed.), 1963, pp. 154–9.

[15] This explanans provides good reasons/grounds for asserting that the ap-

While reasons for action are often deduced from a statement of antecedent conditions and they often refer to some common conceptions of human behaviour, it would be inappropriate to say that they refer to or employ general laws. Unlike the latter, statements about the expected normal or rational behaviour do not postulate a relationship of necessity between the intention and the action, the antecedent situation and the consequent action. Instead of arguing that a particular action had to be performed or that the probability of its being performed was extremely high, they merely suggest that it could have been performed; and if we find that the action is/was performed it makes perfectly good sense to us. It follows from this that reason-action explanations do not seek to predict what an agent would do under certain specified conditions, they explain retrospectively why the decision to act in a particular way makes perfectly good sense. Thus, the general statements invoked in these explanations do not embody laws of the nomological or statistical kind. In fact, reason-action explanations, unlike the covering law model, dissociates explanation from prediction.

While the differences between the covering law model and reason-action explanations are more obvious, one needs to examine the claim that they are similar to singular causal assertions.[16] Like the latter they are asserted retrospectively and do not make any serious claim to predict what will happen or how similar agents will behave when they are placed under similar circumstances. The inability to predict with a reasonable degree of certainty is not considered to be a limitation in either of them. Further, as in the case of singular causal assertions, reason-action explanations assume that when we explain a decision or

---

propriate thing for T under the circumstances was to do A; however, to provide reasons for believing that T did in fact do A, we need to include a further assumption of rational behaviour and argue that:

T was in a situation of the kind C

T was a rational agent at that time

Any rational agent, when placed in situation C, will invariably (or in all likelihood) do A.

[16] Cf. D. Davidson, 'Action, Reasons, Causes', and W.D. Falk, 'Symposium: Action-guiding Reasons', in Journal of Philosophy, vol. LX, no. 23, 1963, pp. 685–700, 702–18.

the choice of an action we do not explain the corrigibility of all such choices in the same way. As such, each of them explains the particular case or performance and does not see its object as an instance of a general kind. On these grounds several theorists argue that reason-action explanations are a special kind of causal explanation and, by identifying the reason for an action, we pinpoint the cause for the action. When we try to explain the actions of an agent we address a causal interrogative. We ask:'Why did A do X to B?'or 'What *caused* A to react in this way?' and in answering these questions we stipulate a causal link between a particular situation, intention and action. When we say that T punished S because S did not attend class, we refer to an antecedent condition whose presence was responsible for the particular outcome. In the process, we accept that if S had not done A, T would not have punished her. Thus, we use causal language and idiom and even assert a counterfactual statement of the form: 'Had S not done C, T would not have done A' or 'Had E not happened T would not have done A'. Theoretically, at least, we allow for manipulation and control.[17]

However, before we accept the claim that reason-action explanations are one form of causal explanation, it would be appropriate to examine if reasons can be considered causes and explanations of actions compared with explanations of events. In the case of those explanations where we refer to the motives and the intentions of the agent to account for his action we only need to reiterate that motives are not happenings and reasons are not events. They are, as Gilbert Ryle points out, states, dispositions, beliefs that may lead to some event but in themselves they are not the right kind of causes.[18] When we speak of a cause we refer to a condition whose presence brought about the given effect by itself or in association with other contingent or contributory conditions. However, when we assert on the basis of our analysis of the existing situation, that the loss of popular support was the reason for the withdrawal of the strike, we do not suggest that

[17] Cf. W.D. Gean, 'Reasons and Causes', *Review of Metaphysics*, vol. 19, September-June 1965–6, pp. 667–88.

[18] Cf. Gilbert Ryle, *The Concept of Mind*, Penguin Books, Harmondsworth, 1980, p. 109.

REASON-ACTION EXPLANATION

the existence of this condition produced the given effect (action). The prevailing condition warrants the action only when it is accompanied by certain perceptions and beliefs. Only when the agent feels that withdrawing the strike would be better than allowing it to fizzle out, because in the case of the latter they would lose the advantage that they have gained so far from the strike, can we say that this condition provides sufficient reason for withdrawing the strike. Similarly, when we explain A's decision to eat his lunch at the salad bar by pointing to his intention to lose weight, we do not suggest that the latter produced the given decision/action (effect). The decision is prompted by some considerations, desires, wants and beliefs, but none of them represents causes. The intention of losing weight is not a condition that causes the given action, and vice versa, the decision to eat at the salad bar cannot be seen as the consequence of this intention.

In addition to this, one finds that the antecedent and the consequent are related differently in the two kinds of explanations. In a causal explanation, one event (antecedent condition/cause) is related to another (effect) through an established general law but in reason-action explanations, the reason is linked to an action logically. When we say that the gas leak was the cause of the fire in the hall, we do not suggest that the gas leak and the fire are related to one another logically. The connection between the two is a contingent one and warranted on the basis of the invoked general law. However, when we explain the action of X by saying that Z humiliated X, therefore X hit Z, we assume and suggest that there is a logical connection between being humiliated and wanting to redress the insult by slapping the offender. The latter is a logical consequence or, at least, a manifestation of the preceding mental state. Besides, as we argued earlier, contingent laws are unnecessary and superfluous in such explanations. In other words, we do not need to refer to any law referring to the actions of all agents similar to X or to X himself that asserts that whenever X or anyone similar to X is in a situation C, he will do A. It is possible to think of a situation where, even with the same provocation, X (or anyone similar to X) may not act in the same manner. However, when we explain the action of X by saying that Z humiliated him, it makes perfectly good sense, and we do not need any further evidence to accept the proposed connection. In the same way when we explain an action by referring to a rule or explaining what kind of act it is, we make an analytical rather than an empirical statement. In response to the question: 'Why did X raise his arm in the class?' when we say that 'X raised his arm to ask a question', we do not refer to the cause of the movement; we do not not suggest that the latter caused him to raise his arm. The statement in the response is of an entirely different order. It explains the action by referring to the rules that govern the use of certain gestures and signs in a classroom. And even if we momentarily accept that the stipulated link between action and motive is causal in nature, one would have to acknowledge that the force of the argument is not causal and that the two do not signify the same thing.

The difference between reason-action explanations and causal explanations is also evident from the difference in the sequence of events in the two kinds of explanations. In the case of the latter, the effect is a consequence of the cause and, even in time priority, it comes after the cause. Rational explanations, on the other hand, are teleological in nature. The desired end state is here seen as the impelling force that catalyses the action. The action (occurrence) is performed for the sake of bringing about the state of affairs that follows or would follow from the performance of that action. Hence, both in terms of logic and time sequence the desired end state is posited first.[19]

Thus, there is considerable difference in the nature and structure

---

[19] An argument of this kind is used by Charles Taylor to explain the nature of teleological explanations. Like the advocates of reason-action explanations, Taylor maintains that the actions of men can be explained only by referring to the purposes for which they are envisaged. Hence, they entail a different form of explanation. However, Taylor's model of teleological explanations is in some respects different from reason-action (rational) explanations. In addition to being empirically verifiable it uses laws, albeit of a form different from Hempel's general laws. Besides, in explanations of this kind the condition for 'an event B occurring is, then, not a certain state of P but that the state of the system S and the environment E be such that B is required for the end G, by which the system's purpose is defined'. (Charles Taylor, *The Explanation of Behaviour*, Routledge & Kegan Paul, London & Henley, 1980, p. 10.) Thus, in teleological explanations, behaviour is not treated as a function of some unobservable entity (purpose/reason); it is instead regarded as a function of some state of the system and its environment, both of which are observable. Moreover, we can establish that the system and the environment required a certain action if the desired/stipulated end is to accrue from it.

of causal explanations and reason-action explanations, and if we equate explanations of actions with explanations of events and treat actions merely as happenings and reasons as causes, we would misunderstand both the concept of action and the notion of reason. Reason-action explanations must, therefore, be considered a distinct and alternative mode of inquiry.

III

Hermeneutic Understanding

Hermeneutic understanding is primarily a way of recovering the meaning of the utterances and performances of historical agents. However, what distinguishes it from other modes of inquiry is the historical nature of its perception, namely, its claim about the historicality of human existence and the plurality of historical worlds. Distancing himself from the Enlightenment conception of history, Herder had, in the mid eighteenth century, argued that the history of humankind is marked by a succession of heterogeneous cultures each with its own distinctive pattern of values, beliefs and linguistic practices. Each culture and life form is unique and complete in itself, hence, it cannot be treated as a stepping stone for another culture.[1] This conception of heterogeneity of cultures, values and modes of societal organization is, within the framework of hermeneutic understanding, coupled with the idea that men, as members of a particular historical world, share the linguistic and non-linguistic practices that characterize their epoch and society. Their actions and utterances express and invoke these practices. Consequently, when we analyse the expressions of the lived experiences of men, we need to study them in the context of their own historical world and with reference to the shared values and practices of their time.

The advocates of hermeneutic understanding maintain that we can

---

[1] J.G. Von Herder, *On Social and Political Culture*, trans. and edited by F.M. Barnard, Cambridge University Press, Cambridge, 1969, p. 188.

understand the actions and utterances of men and recover the link between life and experience embodied in these expressions, only by *reconstructing the life of the other*. When the subject and the object inhabit the same historical world the subject has a direct and almost immediate access to the practices that constitute the object. However, when the subject and the object belong to different historical worlds— as is the case when we study the past or another culture—the subject may invoke the values and norms of rationality that inform his life-world to understand and judge the meaning and significance of the expressions of people whose lives and actions are/were governed by completely different patterns of rationality and thinking. In such cases, to avoid misunderstanding the given expression, we need to systematically construct the historical world of the other.[2]

In our discussion of the different modes of inquiry, it is perhaps important to emphasize that hermeneutic understanding is a way of *understanding*, rather than *explaining*, a given occurrence. The advocates of this view argue that causal explanations (*Erklärer*) is a mode of investigation that is suitable for the *Naturwissenschaften* (natural sciences) where we try to apprehend objects as they are given to us externally through sensory perception. However, when we do not see the object as a phenomenon given in sensation but as an immediate inner reality stemming from and reflecting the lived experience of concrete historical individuals, we need to apply the method of *Verstehen* (Understanding). Only through the latter can we attempt to recover the link between life and expression that is already manifest in the object.

Two arguments are offered by Dilthey in this context: first, the world seen as a material whole and perceived through the senses is just a physical fact that can be explained causally. It becomes the subject matter of the *Geisteswissenschaften* (human sciences) only when we experience human states, give expression to them and try to under-

---

[2] In this framework, the subject like the object is considered to be an historical entity. Just as the object is an expression of the people possessing a particular world-view, similarly, the subject is a human being inhabiting a particular historical world. He is not, in other words, a transcendental ego or a pure consciousness; he is an individual expressing the shared values, beliefs and prejudices of his historical time and society.

stand them.[3] Second, and more important, there are two modes of experiencing reality. Experience for the natural sciences is strictly sensory experience, an analytical minimum stripped, as far as possible, of its anthropomorphic qualities like value, purpose and meaning. But lived experience (*Erlebnis*) that is central to the study of the human sciences explores the world of social and cultural relations and its varied pattern of meanings, values and significance.[4] Thus, the natural sciences and the human sciences represent two ways in which we study and approach the given reality: they reflect the differences in the attitude of the mind towards the object.[5] When we study objects as they are given to us through sensory data—such as size, colour, smell, sound, shape, etc.—we treat them as the subject matter of the natural sciences. However, when we consider the object as an expression of a particular life-world, we include it within the realm of the human sciences.[6] Since an entity becomes an object of the *Geisteswissenschaften* only when we see it as an expression of the people living in a determinate historical time and space, hermeneutic understanding is a mode of inquiry that is particularly appropriate for such disciplines.

[3] W. Dilthey, *Selected Writings*, trans. and edited by H.P. Rickman, Cambridge University Press, Cambridge, 1976, p. 151.

[4] Cf. M. Ermarth, *Wilhelm Dilthey: The Critique of Historical Reason*, The University of Chicago Press, Chicago, 1978, pp. 97–9.

[5] Although Dilthey maintained that the world is present to us only in the form of an interrelated whole, he argued that the different disciplines examine only an aspect of that reality. The *Geisteswissenschaften* represent a group of disciplines that is engaged in the methodological investigation of man both as an individual and as a member of a social and historical world. To put it somewhat differently, they analyse the expressions of lived experience. Exploring the meanings, values and references of the world of social and cultural relations, they analyse objects that can be known from the 'inside'. W. Dilthey, *Introduction to the Human Sciences*, trans. and edited by R.J. Betanzos, Harvester Press, Wheatsheaf, London, 1988, pp. 83–8.

[6] In the natural sciences (when we are dealing with objects that are external to us) we are presented with a set of characteristics such as sound, smell, colour, size and shape, individually. We are not given the inner link between the various characteristics; these links are imposed by the mind. In the human sciences, on the other hand, the link between an experience and an expression is already present in the object and it can be recovered by the subject through the process of understanding.

Indeed, it is the only possible way of recovering the meaning of the different expressions of life.[7]

Expressions of life may be of different kinds, varying from automatic and involuntary to artificial and deliberate. And, they may reveal themselves through facial expressions, gestures and speech, or be externalized in the form of conventional signs, symbols and human action. Spontaneous exclamations, like the clapping of hands or a scream, awaken in us an immediate response and they are relived and recreated in each of us almost automatically. Such expressions of lived experience have the power to invoke in us that which they express, and what we experience at that time is the same as what the person (whom we understand) had experienced. However, experience takes on a different form when we try to make sense of a conversation, a written document and the actions of individuals. Understanding a conversation or a text requires both a knowledge of the spoken language and its grammatical structure, and an analysis of the logical connection between one sentence and another, the tone in which the the word is uttered, the person to whom it is addressed and the question to which it is a response. The act of understanding becomes even more complex and difficult when we address ourselves to the linguistic expressions and practices of people who belong to a historical time and culture quite different from our own.[8] In fact, in all such cases one needs to use the hermeneutic technique of linguistic and historical exegesis to comprehend the meaning of the expression.

The application of the hermeneutic method rests on the assump-

[7] As the *Naturwissenschaften* and the *Geisteswissenschaften* represent two different ways in which the mind approaches a given reality, hermeneutic understanding is a method that is suitable *only* for the *Geisteswissenschaften* or the human sciences.

[8] Dilthey made a distinction between three kinds of expressions in terms of the depth and precision of the insight they give. First, there are those that arise involuntarily out of the lived experience and what they present is more easily felt than defined. These expressions can be suppressed and counterfeigned. Second, there are human actions that are pursued in order to fulfil certain purposes. In these we can discern, to some extent, the purpose from the action itself but immediately we cannot be sure of the validity of our deduction. Third, there are mathematical symbols and conventional signs (e.g., traffic lights and other signals) which can be known unambiguously and with the greatest possible accuracy.

tion that members of a society, at a given moment in time, live and act in a common sphere. We communicate with and understand each other because our performances and utterances invoke this world of shared practices and meanings. We refer to the person standing in front and addressing a room full of rows of young individuals as a teacher and to the other individuals as students attending a class in accordance with the linguistic and non-linguistic practices of our society. We identify one building as a university and another as a theatre, in accordance with the shared norms and linguistic practices of our society. Similarly, when I fold my hands to greet my friend's parents, I invoke the same shared world of meanings and references; and my friend's parents see my action as an appropriate form of greeting in accordance with the same shared practices. Since we inhabit the same world and share a world of practices and references, the meaning of my action is available to them immediately and almost directly. They do not, in other words, need to reconstruct my (the agent's) historical world because they (the hearer or the subject) belong to the same world. However, when we are confronted with the expressions of people who belong to a different culture and historical age, the meaning of their expressions is not similarly available to us; in fact there is, in all such instances, the possibility of dismissing the expression as meaningless, or else, of misunderstanding it by employing contemporary norms and linguistic practices to interpret them. For instance, travelling long distances and waiting for hours in a queue to take a dip in the River Ganges at Hardwar on a specific day may appear as a completely irrational activity to those who do not share the beliefs of a Hindu. It is indeed possible that some people may not, while belonging to the same society, participate in or accept the same Hindu beliefs; they may, in the manner of several foreigners and outsiders, consider this practice irrational. Hence, it may not have the same meaning and significance for them as it does for the practising Hindus, yet, the meaning it has for the latter may be available and accessible to them. When they see others waiting to take a dip in the Ganges, they understand that for the practising Hindus it is as an act of purification. The notion of purification itself makes sense to them and needs no further elucidation. Hence, inhabiting the same world and having access to the meanings and practices of the agents, there is little possibility of their concluding that Hindus bathe only in running water and certain days are set aside by them for a bath in the Ganges. Nor are they likely to conclude that this is the Hindu idea of a community picnic. To put it simply and quite schematically, the meaning of most of the practices and performances of the agents is available to them because, living in the same world, they share internal and external modes of organization.

Three things need to be emphasized here: (a) the existence of shared meanings and practices does not imply that all members of a society *observe* and *perform* the same practices. When a friend folds his hands and says *'namaste'*, I may raise my hand and utter *'adaab'* in response to his action. I may not perform the same action or practice, yet, the meaning of his performative utterance is available to me and, I assume that the meaning of my utterance is similarly available to him. In fact, my action is appropriate only to the extent that I understand the meaning of his action and see it as a form of greeting and he makes sense of my performance in a like manner. And this understanding is possible because we inhabit the same world. (b) Communication among members of a particular society presupposes the existence of intersubjective meanings and understanding invokes just this background of common references. In so far as the expressions of men are an attempt to communicate with others, they must be embodied in a form that is accessible to others. Men must employ shared linguistic and other non-linguistic practices so that other men (to whom these expressions are directed) can grasp the meaning that these expressions had for the agent. To put it somewhat differently, expressions make available to us the inner state of the mind of the agent only when they are informed and constituted with reference to these intersubjective meanings. (c) The 'objective mind' represents this common background of meanings and practices. It denotes the 'manifold terms in which the common background subsisting among various individuals has objectified itself . . . . Its realm extends from the style of life to the forms of social intercourse . . . to custom, law, state, religion, art, science and philosophy . . . . From this world of objective mind the self receives sustenance from earliest childhood . . . . The child grows up within the orders and customs of the family which it shares with other members . . . . Before it learns to talk it is already immersed in that common medium. It learns to understand the gestures, facial expressions, movements and exclamations, words and sentences, only because it encounters them always in the same form and in the same relation to what they mean and express'.[9] The past, and within that, the link between experience and expression can be recovered only in so far as it has survived through such objectifications. In the 'objective mind' the past is a permanently enduring present for us and the relation between life expressions and mental content is always fixed by this shared world. Consequently, it is to this that we must turn in order to make sense of the historically distinct other. The task of the historian is to reconstruct the objective world of the agent. Since the objective world is not given to the historian or available to him 'ready-at-hand', it has to be constituted through an analysis of particular expressions, and when the objective mind has thus been constructed we can understand a particular expression with reference to it.

Linguistic and historical exegesis are techniques by which the historian can reconstruct the life of the other and grasp the meaning of linguistically fixed expressions that constitute the subject matter of the *Geisteswissenschaften*. Minimally, the former requires a familiarity with the rules and canons of the language in which the text is inscribed. To comprehend the meaning of a word we must be acquainted with the norms of grammar and syntax that govern the use of that language but by itself that is not enough. Since words are only indeterminately determinate and they can have different meanings in different contexts, we need to refer to the context in which they are used, i.e., we need to refer to the wider whole of which they are a part. In the first instance we understand the meaning of a sentence by comprehending the meaning of each word, but we can clarify the meaning of each word only by referring to the meaning of the sentence. Similarly, we can understand the meaning of particular sentence by relating it to the paragraph, the paragraph to the essay, and an essay to the whole text. But each text is a part of the wider totality of the texts by that author, and the latter a part of the total discourse going on in that society at

---

[9] W. Dilthey, 'The Understanding of Other Persons and their Expressions', (an essay from *Gesammelte Schriften* VII) reprinted in H.A. Hodges, *Wilhelm Dilthey— An Introduction*, Routledge & Kegan Paul, London, 1949, p. 118.

that time. Consequently, linguistic exegesis involves a continuous movement forward and backward from the part to the whole, from each word to the discourse of that time, till we establish a coherence and concurrence of meaning at different levels.[10] In some ways it involves a process similar to the one by which we understand the meaning of a well-written play where we construct the theme of the play by following each scene and act, and then with reference to the constructed theme, go back to individual scenes and comprehend fully the meaning of particular actions, movements and gestures.

Understanding the meaning of words, symbols and language through systematic exegesis is an essential part of the hermeneutic exercise but, by itself, it is insufficient and must be supplemented with historical exegesis. Every expression—word or action—is a part of the ongoing process of life and it must be related to that whole if we are to understand it at all; that is, it must be placed in the context of the life of that agent, and the latter must be situated in the context of the historical world of the agent. Thus, historical exegesis also entails the recovery of the part-whole relationship. While it does not advocate historical determinism, it suggests that we can understand an expression when we place it in the historical world of which it is a part. The specificity of the agent's experience, the concerns of his time illuminate the meaning of that text and enable us to make sense of the non-linguistic practices that inform the text.[11]

Conceived of in this way, hermeneutic understanding is not a mode of intuitively penetrating the psyche of the author or getting 'inside' his head to capture his inner mental experience.[12] It involves

---

[10] W. Dilthey, 'The Rise of Hermeneutics', in P. Connerton (ed.), *Critical Sociology*, Penguin Books, Harmondsworth, 1976, pp. 104–16.

[11] It is, in other words, different from a contextualist analysis where the analyst postulates a causal connection between the historical milieu and the text and sees the former as an antecedent condition necessarily leading to a particular attitude and expression. For a detailed discussion, see Q. Skinner, 'Meaning and Understanding in the History of Ideas', *History and Theory*, vol. 29, 1969, pp. 39–48.

[12] Although theorists like Schleiermacher had emphasized the need to forge a psychological unity with the author and to relive the moment of creativity, Dilthey displaced psychological exegesis with historical exegesis, and only in this form could it be conceived of as a method for the *Geisteswissenschaften*.

neither an act of emotional projection nor that of empathy. Although Dilthey often referred to it as the process of reliving the life of the other, of forging an identity between I and Thou, nevertheless, transposing oneself into the life of the other did not, even for him, imply that we become the other. When I read the letters and writings of Luther, the writings of his contemporaries, the records of religious disputes, etc., I do not myself become the other. I am, however, able to experience the religious states beyond the possibility of direct experience of a man of our time.[13] Four elements need to be emphasized here: first, while transposing myself into the reconstructed world of the agent, I am fully aware of myself as the subject reliving the experiences of the other. Second, I can relive the experience of the other only by reconstructing, through linguistic and historical exegesis, the life of the other.[14] Third, reliving the life of the other does not entail a duplication of the experiences of the other. Being an exercise of *reconstruction*, it makes available to me the life-world and the experiences of which the object is an expression. Fourth, the meaning recovered through systematic exegesis is one that the contemporaries of the agent would have retrieved from the expression. It is assumed that when I understand the text in the way that the contemporaries would have made sense of it, I recover the 'original meaning' of the text. The meaning is original to the extent that it is precontained in the text and has not been arrived at on the basis of my historical experiences. It reflects the meaning that the text had, in all probability, for its original audience.

The meaning that the text had for the original audience has sometimes been referred to as the 'author's intended meaning'. However,

---

[13] W. Dilthey, *Selected Writings*, pp. 227–8.

[14] Even in those instances where I empathize with the other and relive the experiences of the other, I do not myself become the other. I remain aware of my own separate self and my predicament. For example, on seeing a friend who has been injured tears may roll down my cheek as I consider the hurt and the pain that my friend must be experiencing and what it would be like to be in her position. However, while reliving her experiences I am aware of my separate identity and predicament. I know that what I experience is not my response to the situation in which I might have been placed, nor is it my reaction to the situation in which I am placed. Since it is not the subject's own response to that situation, Dilthey argued that it is an exercise that is subject-related, yet, objective.

as a method of systematic exegesis, hermeneutic understanding does not dwell on the interiority of intentions. It assumes that the text is addressed to other members in society and is, for that reason, encoded in a form that is accessible to others; that is, the basic tools and modes of articulation are derived by the author/agent from the corpus of shared linguistic and cultural practices. Consequently, we can understand the meaning of an expression, just as his contemporaries would, by referring to the shared linguistic and social practices of that time. We can construct the questions that the text addressed and the answer it provides in the same manner. As a mode of inquiry, hermeneutic understanding suggests that to comprehend the meaning of a text is to understand what the author was saying, and what the author was saying or intended to say is what the original addressee would have understood from the text, and the latter can be retrieved by reconstructing the historical world of the author/agent.

Thus, hermeneutic understanding is a particular way of reconstructing and recovering the meaning of a text. As such, it is quite different from *Erklarendes Verstehen* and other modes of *Verstehen* (Understanding) which recover the meaning of an expression on the basis of an established relationship between the stimulus and response[15] or a motive and an action.[16] To put it differently, several theorists refer to the subjective meanings of actions and to the shared world of meanings and references, but not all of them endorse the claims of hermeneutic understanding. Weber, for instance, apprehended the subjective complex of meaning in terms of the *patterns* of motives, goals, attitudes and personalities that are constructed from an analysis of our habitual modes of thought and feeling. He did not concern himself with the historical situatedness of the object and the subject, an attribute that is central to hermeneutic understanding. Similarly, Collingwood assumes that the mind can understand what it has itself created. Consequently, he calls upon the historian to

[15] Theodore Abel, 'The Operation called Verstehen', in J. Bleicher, *Contemporary Hermeneutics*, Routledge and Kegan Paul, London, 1980, pp. 47-8.

[16] Max Weber spoke of the need to understand an action by referring to the motive for an action. The task of the social scientist, he argued, was to show that the established motivational pattern is rational, i.e., it is the most logical and/or the most effective course of behaviour open to the agent.

re-think the *thoughts* of the agent.[17] However, he ignores the her-me-neutic technique of reconstruction and exegesis. Peter Winch, on the other hand, acknowledges the distinctiveness of historical worlds and the historicality of existence. Employing Wittgenstein's notion of 'language game', he maintains that meaningful action is rule-governed. To understand a particular action we must refer to the rules that govern the performance of that practice in a specific society. However, he does not recover those rules through a process of linguistic and historical exegesis. Besides, the claim that every culture has a distinctive language and vocabulary in terms of which men communicate with and understand each other is significantly different from the claim that meaningful action is rule-governed. The former suggests the existence of a world of intersubjective meanings that is continually reconstituted by men in the course of everyday life, while the latter postulates the existence of *rules* that are known to agents and applied by them in the same way in every instance. Consequently, while using Winch's method we need to ask: 'What constitutes rule following?', 'How do I know that I am following a rule?', 'How do I know that I am applying the rule in a manner that conforms to my previous use of that rule?', 'Are there rules about rule following?', 'Do rules govern the performance of every action in society?', 'Is there a rule that specifies the way I walk or sleep?'. More importantly, 'How do I acquaint myself with these rules?', 'Is the process of socialization a way of learning these rules?' etc. In other words, the notion of rule-governed behaviour suggests the existence of commonly acknowledged and known codes of behaviour and it envisages action merely as the endorsement and use of these codes. Consequently, it must consider

---

[17] The events of the past, according to Collingwood, are not 'mere spectacles but experiences to be lived and re-experienced'. (R.G. Collingwood, *The Idea of History*, Oxford University Press, New York, 1976, p. 218.) However, he maintained that we can only re-experience and apprehend reflective actions. As we cannot even relive our own past feelings and appetites, it is not possible for the historian to re-experience these states of the mind; he can only apprehend the acts of thought (reflective action). But in the process of re-enacting the thoughts of the agent he can capture the emotion that survived and was transformed by consciousness into becoming an object for it. See Louis O. Mink, 'Collingwood's Dialectic of History', *History and Theory*, vol. VII, no. 1, 1968, pp. 3–37.

all forms of transgression and deviation from the accepted codes as something other than meaningful behaviour. The notion of intersubjective meanings advocated by the exponents of hermeneutic understanding makes a more limited claim. Instead of arguing that all meaningful action is rule-governed, it suggests that communication assumes the existence of commonly held beliefs and practices. We can understand an expression only to the extent that it is informed by these shared meanings.

As a mode of understanding texts whose meaning is linguistically fixed, the hermeneutic consciousness asserts that the meaning embodied in the written texts and documents has itself to be reconstructed through a process of linguistic and historical exegesis. To put it differently, it suggests that the meaning directly available to us through a reading of the text may be quite different from the meaning that the text had for the agents, particularly when we are analysing the past or another culture. To overcome the possibility of misunderstanding the text, we must bridge the distance between us and the text by reconstructing the life-world of the other. Consequently, a presentation of the assertions and views of the agent is never in itself adequate for understanding the other. Rethinking the thoughts of the other is not, for that reason, sufficient for understanding the other. It may sometimes be the consequence, though never the means of understanding the other.

It is often argued that hermeneutic understanding is neither a mode of inquiry specific to the *Geisteswissenschaften* nor a research programme; as an awareness of the historicality of being, it represents what happens when we understand any object—natural or social.[18] In other words, it is not a method that seeks to recover the meaning hidden in the text by reconstructing the life-world of the agent or the other. In fact, Gadamer argues that re-experiencing and reliving the

---

[18] This conception of hermeneutics is present in the writings of Gadamer and Richard Rorty. In fact, on the basis of these distinctions, Josef Bleicher differentiates between hermeneutic theory and hermeneutic philosophy. For a detailed discussion, see J. Bleicher, 1980, pp. 1–5. Also see R. Rorty, *Philosophy and the Mirror of Nature*, Basil Blackwell, Oxford, 1980, pp. 357–64; and H.G. Gadamer, *Truth and Method*, trans. by Sheed and Ward, London, 1979, Appendix VI, Supplement I, pp. 460–91.

life of the other is neither possible nor desirable. Replacing the works of art to their original context—say, the ceiling of the Sistine chapel—would not give us the same lived experience. Since we do not share those sensibilities, for us it would only be an object of tourist attraction.[19] While a reconstruction of the life-world of the other, even in the minutest possible detail, cannot give us the same lived experience, it enables us to apprehend the connection between different facets of that life; it makes us aware of a way of thinking and living that is, or may be, quite different from our own. Besides, it is the only possible way by which we can open ourselves to the other and grant authenticity to it. While the historicality of existence must also be acknowledged by all disciplines and modes of inquiry, a 'fusion of horizons'[20] of the subject and the object can be envisaged only in the *Geisteswissenschaften*. Indeed, the notion of 'horizon' assumes that the object is also an objectification of the mind. It is perhaps necessary to reiterate that reconstruction is not a means of re-experiencing and reliving the life of the other. It is, at best, a way of penetrating the text and taking cognizance of its otherness. Once we recognize that the subject can neither forget his historical situatedness nor transcend his finitude, the need to reconstruct the life of the other gains even greater significance. Under the circumstances it is the only way by which we can cognize the distinctiveness of the other without translating it in terms that are familiar and accessible to us. In other words, when we recognize that a text addresses us directly and that the words and expressions convey a certain meaning immediately, we need to be cautious of appropriating the text within the horizons of our *Weltanschauung*. Since Gadamer himself suggests that translation represents the paradigmatic case of understanding, we need to assert that translation requires a familiarity with both languages: the language that one is translating from and that into which one is translating. A neglect of the linguistic practices of either would affect the adequacy of the translation. Although translation does not require the recovery of the author's intended meaning, it calls upon the translator to recover the meaning that the text would

[19] Gadamer, 1979, pp. 149–50.
[20] Gadamer characterizes the process of understanding as the 'fusion of horizons'. Ibid., pp. 272–3.

have had for the people who speak that language and share the world of the agent/author.

Without doubt, the text has, and can have, several meanings. As 'discourse fixed in writing' it is, as Ricoeur points out, available to all those who speak the same language.[21] Hence, it is entirely possible that when we read a text we apprehend from it a meaning that it has for us in our world and present predicament.[22] Indeed, a practical and pragmatic interest informs most analyses of the present as also of the past but that does not mean that only those studies that have a direct relevance for us in our present world are significant, or that all historical investigation has an immediate or a direct relevance for us. In so far as reading a text is not just a way of inhabiting a world in which we can 'project our ownmost possibilities', recovering the meaning that is unfolded *in front* of the text is not enough. Indeed it is questionable whether reading serves an inherently critical function; that is, whether it is, as Ricoeur would have us believe, a way of 'opening oneself to the other'. Reading the text with our existing sensibilities and constructing a meaning that it has for us, we are equally likely to affirm our beliefs and prevailing values. Similarly, plural readings of the text may enrich our conception of the text and reveal to us dimensions of the text that were not earlier available to us, but it is debatable whether it would necessarily offer an alternative to our own horizons and way of thinking and living. Reconstructing the life of the other is important to the extent that it presents us, through the life of the other, projects, ways of thinking and organizing that are quite different from our own.

---

[21] Referring to the relative autonomy of the text, Ricoeur argues that the text creates its own audience as it includes almost anyone who can read the language in which it is inscribed. Hence, it transcends the original addressee and is not circumscribed by the intentions of the author or the socio-cultural situation in which it was envisaged. Consequently, it is open to an unlimited number of readings situated in a different socio-cultural context. It has, in other words, the possibility of resonating with new meanings. See P. Ricoeur, *Hermeneutics and the Human Sciences*, trans. by J.B. Thompson, Cambridge University Press, New York, 1981, pp. 197–221.

[22] Understanding, according to Ricoeur, is not an activity by which we project ourselves *into* the text; it is a means of exposing oneself to it and of uncovering that which is unfolded *in front* of the text.

While it is not necessary that it would make us reject our own ways of thinking and living, it would, at least, make us aware of the finitude of our existence and offer us a glimpse of alternative ways of living and thinking.[23]

The purpose of an hermeneutic inquiry is, thus, twofold: (a) it seeks to understand the other, and (b) by making available the life of the other, it opens up new worlds and possibilities to us. Exposure to the other, in this way, serves an inherently critical function. Although it was conceived of by Dilthey only as a method for understanding and recovering the meaning of expressions that are 'permanently fixed in writing', it is today considered to be a way of studying any text, be it a written document, a social practice, individual action or an historical event. We can, for instance, study a magic ritual, a cock fight, a rain dance or the Devi cult hermeneutically by treating each of them as an expression that manifests the beliefs and values of those people, and which can itself be understood with reference to that world-view.[24] Historical events and specific actions of individuals and groups can be similarly understood by recovering the meaning that these performances might have had for those agents. The historian can, by referring to the *Weltanschauung* of the agent, show how each of them perceived the situation and made sense of the actions of the other, and in the process, explain why they decided to act in a particular way. Conceived of in this way, it is a method that has been used by historians, sociologists and cultural anthropologists to make sense of the performances and practices of different communities and tribes that do not share our values of modernity and enlightenment rationality. Historians of contemporary India have used this method to construct the world-view of particular groups, such as the peasantry, to stress

---

[23] Drawing upon the familiar and the known, works of literature and other art forms—e.g. theatre and films—attempt to imaginatively create a world that transgresses the limits set by the present one. Through subtle and sometimes even obvious modes of transgression, they seek to redefine our world and our horizon. Studies of the past and other cultures are, however, different. They do not re-draw the boundaries of our horizon by transgressing its limits. Instead they redefine it by offering a picture of a different life and world-view.

[24] See, for instance, C. Geertz, *Interpretation of Cultures—Selected Essays*, Basil Books, New York, 1973.

the differences in the perception of these groups and the modernizing, rationalist, urban elite that dominated the Congress and the movement for independence. Occasionally, they have used this mode of analysis to comprehend the decisions and actions of those agents and to draw attention to the way in which the policies and the programmes of the national leadership were interpreted and translated by them. A reference to the world-view of these agents enables these historians to inscribe into the text of mainstream nationalist historiography, the actions of a new category of agents, and with it, to displace the dominant voice in the story of the Indian struggle for independence. It becomes, in their hands, a mode of constructing another reasonably different narrative of our past. Outside the framework of Indian historiography, the mode of hermeneutic understanding has been used to show how a clash of perceptions and world-views—for instance, between members of a tribe and the colonizers—resulted in violent confrontations due to the systematic misunderstanding of the actions of the other. Here too, while dwelling on the different ways in which the same movements and actions were understood and perceived by each group, these historians construct parallel narratives of the same event: one, from the point of view of the tribals and another, from that of the colonizers.

The emphasis on plurality of perceptions and the construction of parallel narratives have led many critics to argue that the method of hermeneutic understanding supports and legitimizes unmitigated relativism. Celebrating plurality and difference, it has no place for truth and correct judgement. Under its banner, almost anything goes: all values and systems of belief are equally valid and justified. The existence of slavery is as legitimate and understandable as the belief in the inalienable rights of man. Each is historically specific and, therefore, mutable and transient. Neither can claim to represent the absolute and inviolable order of things. If each is an expression of a distinctive world-view and pattern of internal and external organization, and we must not use our contemporary values and sensibilities to judge other lives and historical worlds, then we must grant each of them—however grotesque, inhuman and unjust they may appear to us—a space to exist in the world. We cannot work for the elimination of some ways of thinking nor banish some beliefs as superstitions. We must accept instead that the belief in goblins is as valid as the belief in atoms and allow both sets of beliefs to exist and be practised. In the context of countries like India, if we were to consider practices like *sati* as expressions of a particular life-world, we would necessarily provide a justification for their continued existence.

The claim that hermeneutic understanding tolerates and justifies retrograde practices rests on the belief that there are certain ways of life and existence that are oppressive and undesirable; also, that our present conceptions of ourselves and modes of social and political organization are better and more adequate for the expression of free-dom, and that freedom defined as the pursuit of one's will without inflicting any physical harm on another, is a more desirable goal of social and individual life. Each of these assertions is in itself quite questionable and it could be argued that the modern world has un-leashed a higher degree of violence and discovered more inhuman ways of torture,[25] but this would only confirm the worst fears of the critics; it would give them further ground to argue that this method is informed by an anti-modern and anti-scientific temperament. It ignores the positive achievements of science and denies the obvious progress that man has made over time in unravelling the secrets of the universe. Consequently, one needs to discuss the issue of plurality of perceptions and relativism a little differently, with reference to the implications of the methodological claims of each of the views rather than to the specific beliefs about modernity.

Accepting the claims of enlightenment rationalism we may privi-lege our modern day conceptions about man, progress and history, and dismiss other conceptions on the ground that they are primitive, untrue and irrational. However, in actual historical practice, we would have to rely on coercive force to banish the other and place in its stead the rational and the true. The latter, established on the basis of force and imposed upon the other, would only establish anew the relation-ship of power and domination with the other. As such, it cannot

---

[25] See, for instance, Ashis Nandy, *Traditions, Tyranny and Utopias*, Oxford Univer-sity Press, Delhi, 1987; Anisuzzam and Anwar Abdul-Melek, *Culture and Thought*, U.N. University and Macmillan Press, London, 1983; and *Indian Philosophical Quarterly*, 1984.

provide the basis of a free and equal society. Besides, force can never provide the basis for effecting enduring change in the structure of society. The latter must come from within the society, either from a recognition of the contradictions in the *Weltanschauung* or from the disparities between our beliefs, expectations and the actual results of our performances. An exposure to other ways of living and thinking can enable us to recognize these contradictions by placing before us alternative conceptions of ourselves and the world. The mode of hermeneutic understanding is important in so far as it reveals to us the finitude of our existence and offers us another world on the basis of which we can question our beliefs and certainties. While it seeks to understand the other in its own terms in order to comprehend its otherness, it serves a critical function, that is, it does not, contrary to common belief, justify each of them in itself. Instead of privileging any one of them in advance, it calls upon the subject to judge and decide for himself the appropriateness and validity of the contending points of view, and to judge it in the light of his awareness of alternative modes of internal and external organization and the possible consequences of each.

The hermeneutic consciousness recognizes the plurality of perceptions that we evidence in history and endorses the claim that there is no way in which we can know the 'thing-in-itself'. Contrary to the positivist claim that the application of the 'scientific method' gives us a mirror image of world and reveals its true structure, it argues that reality is not available to us in neutral observation language;[26] it is given to us only under some description.[27] These claims about the

---

[26] The notion of neutral observation language was rejected subsequently even by the empiricists. Rudolf Carnap and Otto Neurath argued that we do not verify a statement against facts, we merely verify it with other statements that make some assertions about the state of the world. Standing outside the empiricist tradition, Althusser argues that a science does not work on a purely objective given; it works on existing conceptions (Generality I) and provides a critique of the ideological facts elaborated by the earlier practice through its own scientific facts (Generality III). See L. Althusser, *For Marx*, Allen Lane, The Penguin Press, London, 1969, pp. 183–91.

[27] The activity of naming a thing is, within this framework, considered to be an integral part of observation and description. Seeing something implies seeing *that*.

nature of the cognitive process are today endorsed by several philosophers of science who argue that people see the world through a
theoretical 'grid', and looking through different grids/paradigms they
see different things even as they have the same sensory experience.
What appears to a common man as a lamp bulb is to a physicist an
X-ray tube; what Tycho Brahe sees as a pipe, Kepler will see as a
telescope about which his friend Galileo had written to him.[28] If all
experience is mediated and people with different paradigms do not
merely interpret the world differently, but see different things and
inhabit different worlds,[29] then we can no longer claim to have any
access to the world-in-itself. And in the absence of the latter, it is
difficult to assert that a particular paradigm provides a true and
correct representation of the external reality, or that it *corresponds* to
the world outside. In fact, when we accept the claims of the post-empiricist conceptions of science, we are compelled to abandon the cor-

---

According to Hanson, we cannot dismiss the activity of identifying and naming
something as a difference in interpretation. It is not an activity that is secondary
to observation nor does it come after observation; it is a kind of thinking and action
that occurs simultaneously with observation. When I see the figure in the picture
first as an antelope and later, on closer examination, as a pelican, I see different
things. Seeing the figure first as an antelope and then as a pelican involves
interpreting the lines differently but to interpret the lines differently is to see
different things. It cannot be said that I see the same thing in each instance and
only interpret it differently. To speak of a common sense datum in isolation from
the accompanying interpretation is, for this reason, meaningless. N.R. Hanson,
'Observation as Theory Laden', in S. Brown, J. Fauvel and R. Finnegan (eds.),
Conceptions of Inquiry, Methuen & Co. in association with The Open University
Press, New York, 1981, pp. 262–3. Also see F. Suppe (ed.), *The Structure of Scientific
Theories*, University of Illinois Press, Urbana, 1977, pp. 152–7.

[28] N.R. Hanson, 'Observation as Theory Laden', ibid., pp. 262–3.

[29] There is, however, considerable debate on this particular issue. Karl Popper,
for instance, maintains that people with different theoretical frameworks *interpret*
the data differently. That is, they have the same experience and see the same thing
but they categorize and make sense of it quite differently. However, he too
maintains that what we accept as scientific and true is that which has so far
withstood all attempts at falsification. Consequently, it is possible that what we
regard to be scientific today may be falsified tomorrow. Besides, what constitutes
'falsification' itself is something that is decided *not* on the basis of some neutral
observation or experimentation, but by the members of the scientific community.

respondence theory of truth, and with it, the belief that there is a scientific method that gives us a privileged access to reality and truth. The strength of the hermeneutic mode of understanding is that it recognizes that every *Weltanschauung*, like a theoretical grid, provides a disciplinary matrix through which we understand ourselves and the world around us. This conception of the cognitive process may appear to have relativist implications for those who are wedded to the correspondence theory of truth. However, once we accept the untenability of the philosophy of the mirror and abandon the search for foundations, it would not appear as a limitation that must be overcome; instead, it would become a condition of knowledge that must be written into our definition of truth. In other words, the notion of truth would have to be defined in a manner that perceives the historicality of existence and the mediated-ness of experience as conditions of being rather than as obstacles that have to be removed or transcended.

While several theorists acknowledge the temporality of Being, they nevertheless maintain that hermeneutic understanding is justificatory in nature; it only reconstructs the beliefs and values of the agents and does not offer a critique of their perceptions and everyday consciousness.[30] A critique of the agent's self-perception requires the dismantling of all structures of domination and repression that distort and hamper communication. In positive terms it involves, on the one hand, an understanding of the conditions of undistorted communication essential for dialogue and, on the other, a therapeutically guided self-reflection that would make explicit the unacknowledged conditions of action.[31] The problem, however, is that the latter assumes the presence of an analyst who can, on the basis of a metatheory about the self-formative process of humankind, analyse and reconstruct the individual case history and identify the underlying deformations that

---

[30] Making a distinction between technical, hermeneutic and critical interest, Habermas argues that the hermeneutic interest concerns the dimension of interaction and reveals norms of social behaviour that are objectified in ordinary language. The critical interest, on the other hand, involves a reflective appropriation of human life; without it, the interest-bounded character of knowledge cannot be grasped.

[31] J. Habermas, *Knowledge and Human Interest*, trans. by J.J. Schapiro, Heinemann, London, 1978, pp. 308–11.

restrict the patient's self-understanding. Where are we to find such an analyst who has achieved self-consciousness? Who is the neutral person who can be said to have freed himself from the conditions of historical existence that enslave everyone else? Once we recognize that there is no neutral third party who can step outside the game, we would cease to think of emancipatory praxis independently of the conditions that characterize the historicality of existence. Indeed, we would realize that hermeneutic interest cannot be dissociated from the critical interest for it is the only possible way in which we can understand our present predicament and grasp the limitations of our received perceptions. Other ways of life and thinking reveal to us the finitude of our conceptions and present to us alternatives in terms of which we can shape our projects and recognize the limitations and inadequacies of our present conceptions. There is no other external criterion to which we can appeal while judging our contemporary way of life.[32]

Thus hermeneutic understanding is neither justificatory nor relativist in its orientation. However, the most significant limitation of this form of inquiry is that it excludes all forms of causal investigation from the domain of the *Geisteswissenschaften*. It neither reflects upon the conditions of effective history that link certain perceptions with determinate structures of material reality nor does it consider the possibility of comparing and relating aspects of the cultural, religious and economic system. Although it is important to see the latter as

---

[32] When we study the writings of Aristotle, we are presented with a conception of political association (polis) that rests on friendship and community feeling. This conception of civic life presents *both an alternative to and a critique of* our contemporary liberal conception of the state and society. In place of a state that is composed of atomized individuals who are bound to each other only by the mechanism of the market and private needs, it presents the picture of a society whose members are joined together by common values and ideals. Further, its conception of face-to-face relationships and continuous participation by the citizens in the affairs of the state offers a critique of the liberal polity where people participate in the political process primarily when their individual interests are jeopardized, and even then, the people who come together for defending a common interest meet as strangers. This results, quite frequently, in the clash of egos and that itself thwarts collective action and makes continuous participation difficult and ineffective.

objectifications of the mind, yet reified as structures in the world of sensory perception, we can establish patterns of correlations between them by using techniques of causal analysis. Given the domination of the positivist paradigm and its associated conception of empirical social science, it is perhaps necessary to emphasize studies that conceive the social object as an expression. Nevertheless, to exclude the study of causal relationships would only diminish the strength of these disciplines. For instance, the analysis of communal riots as a form of violence or a study of the formation of a community identity over a period of prolonged but sporadic communal violence may offer important insights, but it cannot be a substitute for a study that seeks to examine the relationship between class conflict and communal violence. In other words, it cannot take the place of studies that seek to relate communal violence with determinate social and economic factors. It is indeed paradoxical that a mode of understanding that relativizes our conception of the self privileges in absolute terms the use of a particular method for the study of the human sciences. If the hermeneutic perception were to be applied to methodological issues, we would have to concede the place of other modes of inquiry in the *Geisteswissenschaften*.

There is another contradiction implicit in the hermeneutic mode of understanding. On the one hand, it questions the universalism and scientific rationality of the enlightenment mind. On the other, it postulates a high degree of consensus and homogeneity within a society. It recognizes the plurality and incommensurability of world-views over spatial and temporal boundaries, but it does not seriously consider the existence of different world-views and language games within a given society. To emphasize the possibility of understanding, it refers only to the world of shared meanings and practices and ignores, in the process, the contestation of values and meanings within a society. By assuming that understanding an other in our own society does not pose any serious difficulties, it defines the self so extensively that the other is literally pushed outside the boundaries of our space and time. Indeed, as a part of a community that shares a world of meanings and references, the self becomes conterminous with the boundaries of a particular society, and this notion of community further fosters the picture of distinct worlds that are untouched and uncontaminated by the views of the other. While this conception of societal existence may capture the distinctiveness of tribal societies that had little contact with one another, it cannot be easily applied to contemporary industrialized societies where the other (with ways of life and thinking different from our own) is brought into the very interior of private homes. Besides, this conception of self and community is adequate only for a society that is culturally and ethnically cohesive. In a country like India, the plurality and heterogeneity of cultural, religious and linguistic groups within one contiguous territorial whole makes it difficult for us to speak of a shared world of meanings or a single language game. In fact, the existence of different world-views and language games within one political and territorial whole impels us to reconsider some of the ideas associated with the notion of understanding and misunderstanding, self and the other, embodied in the framework of hermeneutic understanding.

It has sometimes been suggested that the coexistence of several language games necessitates the use of techniques of systematic exegesis to areas and spheres of life that had previously been excluded from the domain of hermeneutic understanding, namely, to groups and societies within our own society. However, this suggestion poses the further problem of identifying the self and differentiating it from the other in a given society. Is the self, in such cases, to be defined in terms of an ethnic, social, religious, cultural, linguistic or economic identity? Since Being is a part of each of these modes of organization, it would have something in common with the members of a group identified on the basis of any of these criteria. The festival of *Onam*, for instance, may have the same meaning and significance for a group of people sharing a cultural context but it may not have the same meaning, or any meaning at all, for people living in a region where there are different cultural practices. Yet, taking a dip in the River Ganges may be a meaningful activity for many people who live in different regions, speak different languages and have diverse cultural practices. Consequently, while analysing any society it is important to specify a particular mode of organization on the basis of which we identify the members of a group and their world of intersubjective meanings because, depending upon the criterion used, we would see them as participants of different language games.

We also need to problematize the belief that the meaning of an expression is evident to the contemporaries who inhabit the same world as the agent. Sharing the same historical world and linguistic practices, the possibility of misunderstanding is considerably minimized when contemporaries read a text, but it is nevertheless questionable whether the text addresses them with one clear voice and whether they appropriate the same coherent meaning from it. As they can enter into a dialogue with the author, they are in a position to clarify the meaning of his assertions but that is all that they can hope for. Even if we were to assume that the meaning of a text can be apprehended by readers who are contemporaries of the author, we need to ask whether reading is merely a way of acquainting ourselves with the other. Since texts frequently make claims about the nature of social and historical reality, do we dwell on the veracity of these claims and judge a text on that ground?

These are questions that are frequently ignored within the framework of hermeneutic understanding, and if we are to consider it seriously as a method for the study of the *Geisteswissenschaften*, then they must be taken into account. These absences do not, however, jeopardize the truth of its historical perception and its conception of the *Geisteswissenschaften*. Indeed the notion of Being, truth and knowledge embodied in the hermeneutic perception must inform all inquiry, and a particular mode of inquiry can be considered adequate only when it incorporates the historical consciousness that informs hermeneutic understanding.

IV

The Narrative Mode

Most critiques of causal explanation began by affirming the distinction between the natural sciences and the human/social sciences. Both reason-action explanation and hermeneutic understanding justified the need for an alternative mode of inquiry by referring to the specific attributes of the *Geisteswissenschaften*. The advocates of the narrative mode also reiterate this distinction. However, what distinguishes them from the others is that they make a further distinction between the social sciences and history. Following Windelband and Rickert, they argue that history is the most 'individualizing and particularizing' of all social sciences.[1] While other disciplines such as sociology, economics, and politics search for generalizations, history concentrates on the unique and the particular.[2] It does not strive to explain why empires decline or candidates win elections; it tells us why the *Roman* empire declined and why candidate *A* won the parliamentary elections in 1989 from constituency C. Unlike the sociologist who might, on the basis of 'case' studies, delineate the *kind* of struggles and conflicts that are involved in the formation of ethnic identities, the historian analyses the actual competition for rights,

---

[1] W. Windelband, 'On History and Natural Science—Rectorial Address, Strasbourg, 1894', trans, by Guy Oakes, *History & Theory*, vol. 19, no. 2,1980, pp. 169–85; and Carl Hinrichs, 'Introduction', in F. Meinecke, *Historism*, traps, by J.E. Anderson, Routledge & Kegan Paul, London, 1972, pp. xvii–Jiii.

[2] This claim is accepted by several philosophers of history, even those who do not support the narrativist thesis. However, what is significant, from our point of view, is that the narrative is privileged over other modes of inquiry because it takes cognizance of the specificity and the particularity of the object.

privileges and resources between different groups in a society at a given moment in time; he studies the formation of a determinate ethnic identity and tries to explain why E_1 rather than E_2 happened.[3] Consequently, it requires a method that can explain the given occurrence without losing sight of its particularity. It requires a method that takes into account the what, when, how and why dimensions.

Hermeneutic understanding and explanations in terms of general laws and reasons are, from the historian's point of view, inadequate because they do not address each of these questions. Reason-action explanations analyse only the actions of the agent; they explain the determinate choices of historical agents rather than the occurrence of the particular event E_1. Hermeneutic understanding also neglects the consequences of the performances and utterances of agents. In fact, it does not even claim to *explain* why something happened or came to be in that form. It takes the expressed form as the object of historical analysis and through it reflects on the nature of the historical being whose life and world-view are manifested in that expression. Causal explanations, by contrast, address the 'why' question. They try to explain why event E_1 occurred but they do this by subsuming the event E_1 under a general law that explains the occurrence of events of the E *kind* by referring to a set of antecedent conditions of the $C_1 \dots C_n$ kind. As a result, they de-emphasize the specificity of the event. While treating E_1 as an event of the E type, they draw attention to those aspects and attributes that it has in common with other such events. Besides, the general laws that they invoke are insufficient for explaining the particular event. General laws tell us the *kind* of thing that could happen but not what did happen. They do not, in other words, rule out

---

[3] Expressing it somewhat differently, Louis O. Mink distinguishes between the theoretical, categoreal and configurational mode of comprehension. The theoretical mode, characteristic of the natural sciences, treats events as an instance of a particular generalization. The categoreal mode, employed by philosophy, comprehends a number of objects as examples of the same category. The configurational mode, associated with history, shows how a particular occurrence belongs to a particular configuration of events like a part in a jigsaw puzzle. Louis O. Mink, 'History and Fiction as Modes of Comprehension', *New Literary History*, vol. 1, 1970, pp. 549–51.

other possibilities of the 'class' or 'membership kind'.[4] For example, a general law would tell us that the roof of a car (of type C) would cave in when it is hit by force f_1; it does not specify the source of that force. Consequently, we can envisage a whole range of actions and possible occurrences that could produce the same effect. The roof could cave in if an electric pole falls on it, if it is struck by a sledge hammer or if people jump on it. In other words, on the basis of the general law we have no way of determining which of these things happened. Thus, when we explain the event by referring to a general law we explain the dent on the roof of *this* car quite indifferently from the way we explain the dent on the roof of *another* car.

To explain what happened in this particular instance we need documentary evidence; we need to examine *what* happened and *how* it happened. We can rule out the possibility of the owner denting the car to collect insurance when we analyse the series of happenings that preceded the denting of the car. If we construct a narrative delineating the series of events and actions of different agents from the time when the car left the hotel (without any dent) with two passengers for the International airport to the time that it came to be dented, we can explain completely why the roof of this car is dented. To put it differently, by analysing *what* happened and *how* it happened we can explain the occurrence of an event in its particularity. The advocates of the narrative claim that if we were to explain the dent on this car by referring to the conditions in which other cars come to be similarly dented, we would lose sight of that which is specific to this situation and that which differentiates the experience of these agents from others'. For instance, it would not be sufficient to say that the roof caved in because it was hit by a sledge hammer or that it was struck by rioters. We would need to identify the person who wielded the hammer and specify who these rioters were and what they were protesting about. In other words, to grasp the uniqueness and particularity of the object we need to explicate the precise configuration of forces at that time, and to the extent that the narrative (unlike causal explanations, reason- action explanation and hermeneutic under-

---

[4] A.C. Danto, *Narration and Knowledge*, Columbia University Press, New York, 1985, p. 240.

standing) does this, it is a mode of explanation that is most appropriate for the subject matter of history.

Implicit in this argument is the claim that the 'why' interrogative can be answered in different ways. Reference to a general law—complete or elliptical, nomological or statistical—is only one way of explaining the occurrence of an event. We can also explain why something happened by delineating the series of intentions, decisions and actions of different agents placed in a determinate historical situation.[5] If causal explanations offer one way of answering the 'why' question, the narrative offers another. Needless to say, the latter is more adequate for analysing the historical object. In fact, it is the only way of apprehending the object historically.[6]

The narrative, it is frequently argued, is a linear and sequential mode of presentation that enumerates events one-after-another in their correct chronological order.[7] While a narrative frequently presents events in a linear time sequence, a serialization of events does not constitute a story. The following sentences—'On 1 December 1990, twenty militants were arrested in Kashmir', 'On 2 December 1990, President Ershad agreed to hold elections', 'On 3 December 1990, the Security Council passed a resolution sanctioning the use of force against Iraq if it does not withdraw from Kuwait by 15 January 1991'—present events in the correct chronological order but they do not constitute a story.[8] Typically, a story is about something: it unfolds

---

[5] See J.H. Hexter, *The History Primer*, Basic Books Inc., New York, 1971, pp. 25-6.

[6] See F.R. Ankersmit, *Narrative Logic*, Martinus Nijhoff Pub., The Hague, 1983; R.F. Atkinson, *Knowledge and Explanation in History*, Macmillan, London, 1978; W.H. Dray, *Laws and Explanation in History*, Clarendon University Press, Oxford, 1970; W.H. Dray, 'On the Nature and Role of Narrative in Historiography', *History and Theory*, vol. 10, 1971; L.B. Cebrik, 'Understanding Narrative Theory', *History & Theory*, vol. 25, 1986, Beiheft, 25, pp. 58-81; and F.R. Ankersmit, 'The Dilemma of Contemporary Anglo-Saxon Philosophy of History', *History & Theory*, vol. 25, 1986, Beiheft 25, pp. 1-27.

[7] See A.R. Louch, 'History as Narrative', *History & Theory*, vol. 8, 1969, pp. 54-70; R.G. Ely, R. Gruner, W.H. Dray, 'Mandelbaum on Historical Narrative: A Discussion', *History & Theory*, vol. 8, 1969, pp. 153-71.

[8] The principle of chronology only provides a negative and not a positive criterion for the concept of narrative. Haskell Fain, *Between Philosophy and History*, Princeton University Press, Princeton, New Jersey, 1970, pp. 285-7.

a series of happenings about an identifiable and determinate object. Reference to one, continuous object provides coherence to the story and offers a basis for identifying all those incidents that are relevant for explaining the event. Nevertheless, a complete record of all the happenings and occurrences related to one object, over a specified period of time, would only constitute a chronicle. As such, a narrative is more than a simple enumeration of events one–after–another in their correct chronological order. It presents every event in the series as a consequence of the mediation of the actions of different agents as they respond to the specific situation in which they are placed. In other words, it delineates a specific situation—with reference to material structures which are themselves defined by the actions of agents—and then shows other agents as reacting to that situation.[9]

While elucidating the notion of an historical narrative, Hayden White argues that a story presents the different incidents in a manner that transforms them into a spectacle with a clear 'beginning–middle–end' structure.[10] Accepting this as the distinguishing attribute of a narrative, several theorists maintain that an event or·a single piece of action is the ideal object for a narrative.[11] A battle, a movement, a revolution, a riot, an agitation are events that can be represented

[9] In the words of W.B. Gallie, it describes 'a sequence of actions and experiences of a number of people . . . . These people are usually presented in some characteristic human situation, and are then shown either changing it or reacting to change that situation from outside'. W.B. Gallie, *Philosophy and the Historical Understanding*, Chatto & Windus, London, 1964, p. 22. Also see P. Ricoeur, *Hermeneutics and the Human Sciences*, trans. by J.B. Thompson, Cambridge University Press, New York, 1981, p. 277.

[10] Hayden White, *Metahistory: The Historical Imagination in Nineteenth Century Europe*, the John Hopkins University Press, Baltimore, 1973, pp. 5-6. Ideally, the beginning must be a point that does not carry us back in thought to all that has gone before. The middle must be the natural sequence to the beginning and must move towards the end, the conclusion or culmination of that action.

[11] To give unity to the drama, Aristotle maintained that a single action (irrespective of its duration) must be the object of the tragedy. (See Aristotle, *On the Art of Poetry*, Clarendon Press, Oxford, 1967, pp. 41-3). This understanding continues to inform most accounts of the narrative. In fact, W.B. Gallie writes that the narrative tries to explain 'some major achievement or failure of men living and working together in societies, nations or some other lastingly organised groups'. (W.B. Gallie, 1964, p. 65.)

narratively. However, if the narrative only requires an identifiable object with a beginning-middle-end structure, we could have a narrative about the life of an individual, the reign of a ruler, the empire of a dynasty, or a specific span of time in the life of a nation or even an institution. Indeed, most historical narratives were traditionally about objects of this kind.

Since the narrative is conceived as a construct with a beginning-middle-end structure, it has frequently been associated with and interpreted as a mode of inquiry that traces the development of an object from its genesis to its present condition. Going back to the origin or the genesis of an entity (the object of historical narrative) represents one way of choosing the starting point (beginning) of the narrative. Even though it is often privileged on the ground that it offers a clear and non-arbitrary beginning for the historical narrative, it must not be seen as an essential attribute of a narrative. To fulfil the requirement of a clear beginning and an identifiable end, narrative accounts frequently examine the happenings related to an object over a specified period of time. The historian, for instance, may study the history of England from 1644 to 1688 or the history of the Indian National Congress from 1930 to 1947. In other words, instead of analysing the object from the moment of its origin (or inception) to its conclusion he may identify the beginning and the end more narrowly and with reference to a specific aspect of the object. He may select a period of time that represents the beginning of an important trend or coincides with the occurrence of an important event or series of events. As and when the identified span of time coincides with the prevalent and accepted periodization of the history of that object, the beginning and the end appear to be quite natural and unambiguous. But this is not always the case. Some objects of narrative discourse do not, even in this limited sense, have a clear beginning or an end. Each of these has to be constructed and determined by the historian. For example, while presenting a narrative account of the transfer of power from the British to Indian hands in 1947, the historian has to determine the starting point of his inquiry: he has to identify a moment that marked, in his opinion, the beginning of that process. He may begin with the Cabinet Mission/on the ground that it came to India with the intention of negotiating the terms of the transfer, or with the coming to power of the Labour government in Britain since they were committed to the principle of self-government. Yet others may begin the narrative from 1942 when the British officials asserted that the principle of self-government would be accepted after the War, or with the pressure placed on the British Government in India by the Quit India movement. Thus, the beginning has to be identified and constructed by the historian. Even while analysing an event which has an identifiable beginning and end—for example, a communal riot—the historian would need to go beyond the ostensible starting-point of the riot. Minimally, he would have to refer to the actions of different agents and to the situation preceding the riot. For example, if the riot had occurred in the wake of the assassination of a leader, then to link the antecedent and the consequent events and to explain why the violence was directed against a particular group/community, the historian would need to refer to some of the incidents and actions that went into the shaping of group identities in that society. A reference to the context of the riot would, in any case, take him beyond the beginning of that event.

Given these considerations the narrative must not be seen as a mode of inquiry which traces the growth and development of an object from the point of its origin to its eventual conclusion. In fact, the narrative questions the idea that an event has a pre-given and identifiable beginning and end. Other than the fact that the narrative frequently describes objects in terms of subsequent happenings,[12] it suggests

[12] Making a distinction between action sentences and narrative sentences, Danto points out that the latter do not merely describe what a person is doing, they describe the action by referring to a subsequent event or action. The narrative sentence does not merely speak of 'John planting roses', it refers to John planting *prize-winning* roses. Thus it redescribes the past event in the light of subsequent ones which were unknown to the actors, at least at the time of performing that action. In all such sentences the action is described by a predicate that links two time-separated events and provides a time description of the earlier event/action. The essential difference between an action sentence and a narrative sentence is that the former uses 'project verbs' of the form: 'B is R-ing' (*John* is *planting* roses/ *repairing* a radio) but it does not logically require that the latter event should actually have occurred: whether John was successful in repairing the radio, whether the roses planted by him grew and blossomed is of no consequence because it does not in any way impair the truth of the statement. However, in a narrative sentence,

that what happened can be understood only with reference to the consequences generated by that event. Instead of privileging the account of the contemporaries, it maintains that the event is not exhausted by its point-like effervescence. Even though we identify an historical event by that sudden outburst, several happenings, spatially and temporally distanced from that occurrence, are so closely related to it that they must form a part of that event. For instance, we may identify a communal riot by the violent clashes that are witnessed, but the subsequent occurrence of violence in another part of the country, or the demand for a separate homeland, may also be seen as incidents that are constitutive of that event. These later developments not only redefine the boundaries of that event, they illuminate the nature of the event and reveal aspects of it that were not available to the contemporaries who lived through the period of the violent outburst.[13]

Hence, an historical narrative is neither an account of an object from its genesis nor a simple serialization and description of events one–after–another. It is essentially a form of explanation in which the explanandum (the event to be explained) follows from and appears as a consequence of the actions of individuals and groups placed in some determinate historical situation. Although the narrativists assert that the actions of individuals make a crucial difference to the nature of the

---

the project verb (R-ing) is treated as a 'future-referring' term which must actually occur if the sentence is to be regarded as true.

Two conclusions follow from this: (i) by using narrative sentences, the historian does not describe actions as witnesses might see them; he visualizes them in connection with later events and as parts of temporal wholes. (ii) The narrative discourse is intrinsically incomplete. Since it redescribes that past event in the light of subsequent ones, it stipulates that the whole truth of the event can be known only after the event has taken place.

See A.C. Danto, 1985, pp. 143-81, 346-8; and P. Ricoeur, *Time & Narrative*, vol. I, trans. by Kathleen McLaughlin and D. Pellauer, University of Chicago Press, Chicago, 1984, pp. 143-9.

[13] To say this is not to undermine the significance of the experiential record. Indeed, experiences are often presented by agents in the form of a narrative, and these represent an important record for the historian. Nevertheless, it is important to make a distinction between the narrative constructed by the historian in his endeavour to explain a particular occurrence and an account presented by a person who lived through that historical moment.

precise occurrence, what needs to be emphasized is that they neither ignore the objective material structures nor claim that the occurrence can be explained in terms of the actions of the individuals alone. They acknowledge that men act in determinate situations: their actions are a response to the situations in which they are placed and can, therefore, be understood only with reference to that historical situation. The actions are, in their view, circumscribed by the configuration of external forces. The latter define the boundaries and parameters of possible choices and actions; they offer certain options to the agents and determine the possible outcome of the performed actions. Equipped with this understanding that the historical event cannot be studied and explained only in terms of the actions of people, the narrative moves to and fro from the text of the actions of men to the context in which these actions are envisaged and performed. Consequently, it combines the dispositional element with the episodic and the structural, and the delineation of the historical world of the agents and the specific situation in which they are placed form an integral part of the narrative form of explanation.[14]

It is perhaps necessary to reiterate that a reference to the structures that characterize a situation is essential for situating the main action, comprehending the choices available to the agents and for explaining the eventual outcome of those performances. Consequently, an analysis of the nature and function of these structures is an important concern of the narrativists though, from the point of explaining the event, it is even more important for them to refer to the manner in which these structures supplement and constrain each other and, in the process, constitute the determinate historical moment. Thus, while constructing a narrative historians refer, at one level, to the conjunction of external material conditions along with the actions of men, and at another level, allude to the historical conjuncture or the precise structuration of different forces at that time.

---

[14] While this is the general pattern of a narrative explanation, the emphasis on the structural and the dispositional aspect varies from narrative to narrative. For a long time, historians described the context primarily in terms of antecedent happenings and actions and did not refer to structural configurations, but contemporary narratives often present the situation as a moment or conjuncture of determinate material and ideological structures.

As such, the narrative mode of explanation has two distinct attributes: (a) it emphasizes the 'what' and 'how' dimensions and explains the occurrence of an event by elucidating how something
happened; (b) it explains how something happened by referring to the
complex of antecedent conditions and actions of individuals. The
causal mode of inquiry explains why something happened by pin-
pointing some antecedent condition whose presence ensured the occurrence of the given event. The condition may be a necessary moment
of a complex of conditions which is collectively sufficient for the result
or it may be one of the many causal conditions which is in itself
sufficient for bringing about the event. The task of the investigator,
accordingly, is to identify which of the possible causal conditions was
present at that time and what were the other conjuncts and disjuncts
of that condition. In each of these instances, causal explanations try to
demonstrate 'why necessarily' something happened. The narrative, on
the other hand, explains how a particular event 'could possibly' have
occurred.[15] Instead of considering a particular event as an instance of
a general law that manifests an invariable and necessary relation
between the antecedent condition and the consequent event, it acknowledges that similar antecedent conditions do not always lead to
or result in the occurrence of the same event. Famine in one region may
result in the decimation of the population but in another place it may
lead to the migration of the population to a neighbouring area. Given
the variation in the consequence, it is important to see what did
actually happen instead of postulating the 'class' of things that might
have happened. Even when similar antecedent conditions are followed by similar events it is more important to see how, and in what
manner, these conditions shaped and influenced the consequent; what
kind of action was envisaged in those conditions and in what way the
conjunction of the two resulted in that particular occurrence. It is not,
for instance, enough to know that the bourgeoisie always betrays the
movement for national liberation; the pertinent thing is to analyse the
manner in which the bourgeoisie actually betrayed the particular
movement for independence. In other words, it is far more meaningful
to examine just how a particular event occurred and to determine what

15 W.H. Dray, 1970, p. 161.

sort of event it was: for example, if it was a movement for national liberation or a bourgeois revolution; a fulfilment or a betrayal of the promise of freedom. It is assumed that in the process of answering 'what' happened and 'how' it happened, we would be able to explain and account for the occurrence of that determinate historical event. For example, we can explain the annexation of state 'S' by 'Y' in the following manner: Y formed an alliance with Z and the two jointly attacked 'S' from the North and the West in the year 'a'. To fight against the joint attack of Y and Z, S divided its troops and sent a small contingent of men (S_1) in the West, leaving S_2 to fight the offensive launched by Y in the North. In the following two days of battle, the troops of Z surrendered in the West to S_1 but S_2 met with heavy casualties. S_1 was summoned to join S_2 but by the third day most of the men of S_2 were either killed or injured; they decided to lay down their arms since S_1 was unable to reach in time. Consequently, Y proclaimed S as a part of its empire.[16]

Conceived in this way, the narrative constitutes an independent and autonomous form of explanation quite different from causal explanations. Unlike the latter it does not explain an event by subsuming it under some general law; it assumes instead that an historical event is a 'unique particular'. This assertion has led some theorists to compare the narrative with singular causal assertions which also explain a particular event by identifying the causal condition that was operative in the instance under consideration. Like singular causal assertions, the narrative explains an event retrospectively but the similarity between the two ends there as the narrative does not ask: 'what C_1 caused E_1?' (e.g. the defeat of S by Y). It does not analyse whether the cause for the defeat of S in this instance was the superior military strength of Y, the military alliance between Y and Z or the inability of troops S_1 to reach the North. To put it differently, it does not analyse whether any one of these conditions could by itself have produced the same effect, whether any of these is a necessary moment of a complex of conditions

---

[16] One has deliberately chosen a narrative which only describes events and actions one-after-another to show that in the process of answering 'what' happened and 'how' it happened we can also answer the question: 'Why did X happen?' Needless to say that, to be an adequate and convincing narrative, it would need to refer to the configuration of structures, instead of merely detailing the sequence of events.

that was jointly sufficient but in itself unnecessary for the effect. It argues instead that the defeat of S can be explained only by referring to the *series* of antecedent conditions and actions. Sociologists and historians refer to this series as a single causal condition or minimal sufficient condition. However, this conception poses serious difficulties. Other than the fact that it is difficult to conceive of the structural and the intentional element as conjunctive conditions of a single minimal sufficient condition, such a characterization would eliminate the notion of overdetermination from the discourse on causation. If the conjunction of different elements of the series is seen as one single minimal sufficient condition then we can no longer speak of a situation where two or more minimal sufficient conditions are present simultaneously. Besides, if we were to designate all the happenings and actions preceding the event as conditions that were jointly sufficient for the given effect, then the minimal sufficient condition designated as the cause would only redescribe the situation that existed: it would make the notion of causation a formal and empty concept. Recognizing these difficulties the narrative does not explain an event by identifying conditions that were responsible for producing it; nor does it, for that matter, explain by alluding to general laws. This attribute further differentiates the narrative from singular causal assertions. Advocates of the latter assume that all explanations refer, at least implicitly, to laws though they do not always consider it necessary to 'dredge up' those laws. The narrativists, by comparison, claim that laws are *not* the essence of explanation. They may be, and sometimes are, used to support an explanation but they are superfluous for narrative explanations of the form: '*A* because *B*'. When we say that '*X* was included in the cricket team that would be touring Australia because he hit a century in two tests when he played against the Australian team last year' or that 'the student union withdrew the strike because they felt that the student community might not support them as the end-term examinations were only a month away', we do not need to refer to any general law to complete the explanation. The explanatory potential of the explanation does not, in such instances, depend upon the veracity of a general law that may be implicit in the explanation.

Some advocates of the narrative, however, maintain that it uses laws of a special kind—laws in which the required initial conditions have to be satisfied in a sequence. While they agree that there is no one single general law that can cover the change that is being explained in the narrative, nevertheless, they believe we can conceive of a law in which the occurrence of the event is dependent on the fulfilment of temporally distinct initial conditions in the stipulated order.[17] In disciplines where the nature of the object makes it difficult even to ascertain and establish a necessary and invariable relation between two discrete events or sets of conditions, the urge to formulate complex historical laws can only be considered a theoretical fantasy and an instance of misguided optimism. In any case, if we were to identify the specified series of conditions and happenings it would still be meaningless to refer to them as a law because, applying only to the case in hand, it would be a unique and singular series.

In the debate on the nature of an historical narrative it is perhaps necessary to emphasize that the narrative does not merely describe what happened. Although it does not investigate a problem that refers to a class of events, it nevertheless explains the determinate occurrence by revealing the nature of determination. Even though it does not refer to general laws, it specifies the nature of the concrete by revealing the connection between a particular situation, action and eventuality. Unlike a causal explanation it attributes causal efficacy to a particular conjuncture; it shows the precise connection between particular units and structures to characterize the historical situation, then, with reference to the specific actions of different agents, it shows that what did happen, happened because the situation was what it was. It does not refer to a necessary and sufficient antecedent condition because it realizes that in a particular figuration, a range of effects and courses of actions is possible. Therefore, it maintains that the consequent can be explained retrospectively only by referring to the specificity of the situation.[18] Thus, it does not see the contingent occurrence as the

---

[17] We can have laws that suggest that if C^0 occurs at time t_0 and $C^1 \ldots C^n$ at time $t_1 \ldots t_n$, then E will occur. That is, we can have laws of the form $(C^1_{t_0}, C^2_{t_2} \ldots C^n_{t_n}) \rightarrow E$.

Danto refers to these laws as 'historical laws'. The essential difference between them and the Hempelian general laws is that they refer to a process rather than a single event. A.C. Danto, 1985, p. 254.

[18] Althusser's conception of structural causality is important for our under-

logical, necessary or the only possible outcome. Instead it links the different incidents and happenings in a manner that makes the consequent highly probable. Using this notion of determination and contingent actuality, the narrative has the advantage of being a non-reductionist form of explanation. While it emphasizes that which is unique or particular to that situation, it takes cognizance of the possible continuities and similarities at the level of structures.

At this juncture it is equally important to note that the narrative as a form of explanation is quite different from rational or reason-action explanation. Although it does sometimes refer to the mental states, thought processes and purposes of people participating in the drama, it does not explain a particular occurrence in terms of the dispositions or intentions of the agents. Nor does it explain (contrary to Danto's argument) by demonstrating that something happened to 'X', therefore, he decided to act in a particular way. It attempts instead a 'rational *re-construction*' of what did happen,[19] and through it, the historian seeks to reconstitute the past.[20] In other words, the narrative represents a linguistic and intentional construction of the object, that is, of what did happen. To say this is not to suggest that the construct (narrative) is artificial or something unreal. It refers to real historical events, the only difference being that several events occur simultaneously or in quick succession but not all of them are included in the narrative. What goes into the construct depends on the nature of the plot and the questions that the historian asks.[21] However, every such

------

standing as it takes cognizance of just these features and approximates, at least theoretically, the notion of determination and causality used in the narrative.

[19] This assumes the active role of the subject (the historian/narrator) in constructing the narrative.

[20] Just as objects are constituted by the consciousness, similarly one can say that the past is constituted by the historian.

[21] It is assumed that the historian has to take the initiative to decide what he wants to know and the question that he formulates would guide the choice of material. This does not, however, imply that the inter-connections are imposed on the material arbitrarily. It merely suggests that the historian finds means of compelling the record to speak. The historian uses texts, passages, etc. about something different to answer the precise question that he has decided to ask. As Collingwood pointed out, the historian brings with him the 'second record' (total consciousness) which aids his deciphering of the first (i.e. available documents).

construction is an attempted reconstruction of what probably did happen or at least it is a synthesis of what might have happened. Even though the historian draws upon the available documents and information, the picture painted is essentially a reconstruction. It is a reconstruction for two important reasons: first, since each record or survival is an object without any specific or exhaustive reference, it can be used in constructing a variety of historical situations, each of which addresses a particular question about the past.[22] Second, from the available records and documents the historian can know the precise event that occurred, but historical *situations* have to be constituted by the historian in such a way that we can visualize and understand a particular condition of human existence coherently, in all its complexity and intricacies. For this reason, the historical event depicted in the narrative is a reconstruction of an occurrence or a situation that has not itself survived. As an object that is subsequently reconstituted by the historian from the survivals of the past, the narrative is a 'representational picture' and not an imitation or copy of the past. Unlike a copy, which is only a means of communicating what is copied, the picture is not the same as what is represented in it: it does not exist in order to cancel itself out. It is important in itself and it is significant to see how what is represented in it is actually presented. Moreover, as a representation or a picture, its relation to the original is quite different from that of the copy. Unlike the latter, it has an independence which in turn affects the original; that is, it is through this representation that the original makes its presence.

What needs to be emphasized is that the narrative uses a different conception of objectivity and truth. By stressing the 'constructionist thesis'[23] the narrativist is not questioning the truth content of the

---

Cf. R.G. Collingwood, *The Idea of History*, Oxford University Press, Oxford, 1976, pp. 241-8.

[22] The survivals of the past, according to Oakeshott, must be regarded as performative utterances that belonged to a bygone present. As practical engagements of that age they were addressed to contemporaries and not to prospective or future historians. See M. Oakeshott, *On History and Other Essays*, Basil Blackwell, Oxford, 1983, p. 55.

[23] See L.J. Goldstein, *Historical Knowing*, University of Texas Press, Illinois, 1976, pp. xi-xxvii, 183-216; and L.J. Goldstein, 'History and the Primacy of Knowing',

narrative but only suggesting that knowledge of the 'real' past or what actually happened (the thing-in-itself) without any reference to the subject or the knower is not available to us. For him the historical narrative is an intentional object, but its ontological source is the real events of history and it is based on evidence and documents of the past that are available to us.[24]

Even though in plotting the chain of events the historian is not required to re-live the experiences of agents or to empathize with them, nevertheless some historians believe that they must reconstruct what had happened in a manner that will 'describe for the stay-at-homes, the sights, sounds and flavours of the place visited'.[25] If the narrative is supposed to provide a 'proxy-experience' we may prefer an account for its coherence, vividness, familiarity or completeness. Apart from the aesthetic criteria, a narrative may be challenged by the results of further inquiry into the elements from which it was initially constructed. Eventually, a convincing narrative is one which can improve upon the existing accounts of the same occurrence and withstand the criticism of other contemporaries using the same or available evidence and information. Implicit here is the belief that the historian does not and cannot approach his material with a blank mind. Before he approaches or confronts his material he has a preconception of it which is based on the existing historical accounts of that period of time.[26] However, in the process of reading the sources (or the material) these preconceptions often get revised and thus another narrative is constructed, one which is able to fill the gaps in the available accounts or bring to light a previously neglected dimension. In this manner, through the narrative, the historian enters into a dialogue with the past and with other historians.

It is sometimes argued that the narrative is fascinated by the

---

History and Theory, vol. XVI, no. 4, Beiheft, pp. 29–52.

[24] Oakeshott, of course, carries the argument further and differentiates the past from its survivals, an event from the historical situation and the constituted historical event.

[25] A.R. Louch, 1967, p. 60.

[26] In other words, the historian does not begin with virgin historical records but with information processed by the accounts of other historians. This forms the background information with which he goes to the primary sources.

unique and the unrepeatable; it assumes that significant changes are point-like ones that affect individual lives due to the brevity of their suddenness. Consequently, it focuses on 'short, sharp and narrow vibrations' (the events) and neglects the *longue durée*. Though it is difficult to deny that the gentle and almost changeless rhythms that characterize structures over time are not generally the object of an historical narrative, nevertheless, the event is a variable of the plot, and it need not for that reason be a brief or sudden explosion. The Mediterranean, for example, is a narrative of the 'gradual and slowed down march of the major event: the retreat of the Mediterranean from general history'.[27] In fact, one needs to reconsider the posited dichotomy between structures and events. As Paul Ricoeur points out, the event appears in the midst of structures in at least two ways: (i) different structures change at a different pace and the dissonance itself becomes event-like; (ii) the exchange between the numerous zones of civilization also constitute quasi-point-like phenomena which do not mark a civilization on every level at the same time. Consequently, it is perhaps a little inappropriate to postulate an unbridgeable divide between structures and events and to argue that the narrative neglects the more permanent structures and deals only with the fleeting event.

Critics of the narrative also argue that historical accounts are different from stories. Based on available documents and authentic historical data, they are not the products of imaginative representation. The characterization of all stories as works of fiction is quite untenable as we do have stories that are empirical, historically real and based on a considerable degree of empirical research.[28] Yet, there are significant differences between an historical account and a story. In a literary narrative, action is generally imputed to agents who can be designated by a proper name, identified and held responsible for their actions. The historical narrative deals with objects of a different kind: it refers to collectivities such as nation, society, civilization, social class, mentalities, etc., that represent a different order of generality. Besides, the writer of a literary narrative may describe events, actions and

[27] P. Ricoeur, 1984, p. 217.
[28] See R. Scholes and R. Kellogg, *The Nature of the Narrative*, Oxford University Press, Oxford, London, 1975, pp. 13–14.

experiences of a number of people, real or imaginary. The historian, on the other hand, does not dwell in the world of fiction, nor does he invent what he narrates; rather, he tries to establish what did happen on the basis of available historical records. Consequently, the historical narrative is essentially a result of careful research and investigation. It is born as inquiry and the condition of ignorance and unreflective activity that characterizes the following of a story are not representative of the historian's procedure.[29] Moreover, in the narrative the 'end' is not known to the reader in advance. Even though each scene and chapter contribute to the next as also to the main action, the narrative conclusion can be 'neither deduced nor predicted'.[30] Consequently, the reader/audience is 'impatient to see the sequel'.[31] However, the air of suspense that characterizes the following of a story is absent in our reading of an historical account. The conclusion (end) of a particular process or course of action is usually known to the reader of history. Even while writing about societies and civilizations quite different from our own or those about which relatively less information is available, the historian does not try to generate a sense of mystery, nor does he keep us waiting anxiously for what is going to happen.

Setting aside the question of the relationship of the reader to the text, we need to consider other differences between history and the genus story. While both of them explain by referring to structure, determinate situation, and agency, yet the relative emphasis and the treatment of each of these elements are considerably different. In a story the context is, in a manner of speaking, supplementary, separate and autonomous. It forms the backdrop against which the main action of the drama is enacted.[32] In history, an accurate and authentic presentation of the context is as, if not more, important than the delineation

[29] Although it is difficult to accept Mandelbaum's conception of the narrative, on this point there can be little dispute with him. See M. Mandelbaum, 'A Note on History as Narrative', *History and Theory*, vol. VI, 1967, pp. 413–19.

[30] P. Ricoeur, 1981, p. 277.

[31] S.H. Butcher, *Aristotle's Theory of Poetry and Fine Art*, Dover Publications Inc., New York, 1951, p. 288.

[32] See H. Ruthrof, *The Reader's Construction of the Narrative*, Routledge & Kegan Paul, London, 1981.

of the action. A description of the context—that is, the structures that constitute it, their nature, function and the manner in which they are related to each other—is an important task of the historian. Unlike the narrator who refers to the context primarily for situating an event or an action, the historian is interested in painting a probable and acceptable picture of the other civilization and historical time. Consequently, what is in the narrative merely a depiction of background scenery is, in history, constitutive of the event and determines the possible courses of action.

Linked with this is the difference in the concept of time used in history and the general narrative form. Conceptualizing time, like Leibniz, as an order of succession, the narrative presents events chronologically. The historian also sees events occurring in a linear time sequence but he supplements this notion of linearity with a concept of historical time. Consequently, he does not see events stretched continuously and endlessly through the passage of time; instead, he splits time into clusters—epochs and eras—each of which is characterized by specific social, economic, political and ideological structures. It is in the context of such units/structures, common to an historical time, that the historian locates his narrative. In other words, a linear sequence of events is placed within a determinate historical time. The latter possesses the quality of linearity but at the same time denotes a whole, a totality marked by the specific relationship of the different particulars within it. The historian is concerned both with the totality and its particular moments and expressions. Each particular reflects the totality or, to use the Hegelian terminology, contains universality within it, and as a concrete and determinate expression of universality it is also its externality and reflection.[33] Hence, the historian is not concerned with the particular—unique and singular—*per se*, but with the particular-in-totality, or to use another phrase, with the difference in the process.

Two other qualifications may be made regarding the nature of the historical account. Generally, the narrative provides a proxy-experience. In it, as also in a play, the spectator—living in the present—easily

[33] G.W.F. Hegel, *Logic: Being Part One of the Encyclopaedia of the Philosophical Sciences*, trans. by Findlay, Clarendon Press, Oxford, 1978, pp. 226–30.

identifies himself with the character (usually the hero) whose fortunes he follows. History on the other hand cannot, in fact does not, try to duplicate the experience of agents living in another time and place. Armed with a sense of historical time, it recognizes that re-living the life and experiences of the other is neither desirable nor possible. Moreover, a story/narrative usually serves a cognitive and moral function. By depicting the probable (i.e. what happens given a particular configuration of forces) the author converts facts into truths; he rises above the common, everyday course of things and represents the universal, permanent and eternal truths, free from the elements of unreason which disturb and even obstruct our comprehension of real events and human conduct.[34] History, unlike a story, is not explicitly concerned with the moral aspect although it does sometimes, in the course of weaving together and presenting anew what had happened, comment on and judge the desirability and correctness of a particular perception, decision or course of action. Nor does it try to unveil the universality underlying all particularity. Instead, it is concerned primarily with the empirical, with what 'is'/'was' and not what might have been. Of course, the concern for the factual is motivated by a practical interest, by the desire to understand ourselves, our present and the way we came to be what we are. Hence, in an historical inquiry, a concern for the cognitive and the practical interest substitutes the concern for the moral and the eternal.

Thus, the historical narrative is a special kind of story with its own distinct attributes. To differentiate it from some of the ideas commonly associated with a story, it may be better to describe it as a mode of configuration in which the historian presents a picture of the past and shows what happened, how it happened, and, through that process, why it happened. Using the available records, he redraws the pattern of concrete relationships and interactions, thereby re-figuring the pre-figured world and delineating what had in all likelihood happened.

[34] S.H. Butcher, 1951, pp. 18–94.

V

Some Considerations on Method

Two conclusions follow from our discussion of the nature and structure of causal explanations, reason-action explanations, hermeneutic understanding and the narrative: first, each of these four modes of inquiry represents an independent and autonomous form of explanation; second, the 'why' interrogative can be answered in different ways and causal explanations present one way of answering that question. Reason-action explanations and the narrative provide alternatives to the causal mode of inquiry: indeed, they constitute non-causal forms of explanation. This conclusion may be difficult to accept because we habitually equate the explanation of a phenomenon with an inquiry into its causes. We assume that the purpose of every scientific investigation is explanation and an explanation is complete only when it successfully identifies that 'C (causal condition) caused/will cause E (effect)'. Consequently, we do not even envisage the possibility of a form of explanation other than causal. In fact, to speak of a non-causal form of explanation appears to us to be anomalous, even a contradiction. However, when we recognize that reasons are *not* causes and that the narrative is not an inquiry into the causes of an event, we can distance ourselves from this belief that we have inherited uncritically from the Enlightenment. Recognition of alternative modes of explanation becomes, in this context, a necessary prerequisite for a critical appraisal of the beliefs that inform our thinking on scientific investigation and knowledge.

Causal explanations, reason-action explanations and the narrative have been considered alternative modes of explanation because each of them conceives the object of analysis differently, and consequently, asks different questions. Ostensibly all of them seek to explain some determinate occurrence and ask: 'Why did E happen?' Yet what they look for in their attempt to explain that occurrence is quite distinct. Causal explanations, for instance, look for a condition whose presence was crucial for the occurrence of E. Hence, to answer the question: 'Why did E happen?', they ask: 'What *conditions* caused/will cause E?' Reason-action explanations look for reasons, beliefs and interests of the agent to explain the performance of a particular action. Such explanations analyse actions and explain an event in so far as it is the outcome of that action. They do not, in other words, see the occurrence merely as an event in the physical world; they consider it to be the consequence of purposeful actions. Consequently they ask: 'What R (reasons/interests) prompted A to do E?' The narrative, on the other hand, refers to the dialectic of structure and agency and asks: 'What *situation* and series of *actions* resulted in the occurrence of E?' In this way, each of them makes sense of the occurrence (explanandum) quite differently; and this difference in their approach is reflected in the dissimilarity of the questions they ask.

Thus far, one has only stressed the difference between causal explanations, reason-action explanations and the narrative because the distinctiveness of the hermeneutic method is more readily conceded. Most people accept that it conceives the object of inquiry differently and represents a non-causal form of explanation. However, since they perceive it as a mode of understanding rather than explanation, they are able to dismiss the claim that it represents a reliable and objective mode of inquiry. In their view it merely justifies what happened while the important thing is to explain why it happened. The distinction between *Verstehen* and *Erklärer* had been made by Dilthey himself and, like the critics of *Verstehen*, he too equated explanation with causal explanation, and the latter with the method used in the natural sciences. Nevertheless, understanding was, for him, a way of apprehending and making sense of the objectifications of the mind: it represented a mode of analysing the 'what' and 'why' dimensions, albeit in a manner quite different from causal explanations.

Consequently, hermeneutic understanding must be placed

alongside other modes of explanation though each must be seen as addressing a different question. In other words, they must not be seen as four alternate ways of answering the same 'why' question. Unlike the causal and narrative forms of explanation, hermeneutic understanding and reason-action explanations do not ask 'why did E happen?' They address the question 'why did X do Z?' or 'what was the meaning of Z for X?' In fact, even this characterization of reason-action explanations and hermeneutic understanding is less than adequate. It enables us to differentiate them from causal explanations and the narrative, but it flattens out the differences between them. In fact, it would be difficult to say that reason-action explanations and hermeneutic understanding present two distinct ways of answering the question 'why did X do Z?' because both would refer to the agent's avowed reasons or perceptions. And we would not, on that basis, realize that the agent's reasons and assertions are analysed and understood differently in the two modes of inquiry. Unlike reason-action explanations, the hermeneutic mode makes sense of the statements and avowed reasons of the agents with reference to their shared world of intersubjective meanings and maintains that what appears to us, from their statements, to be reasons for an action may not, in the original historical context, be sufficient for explaining a particular performance or utterance. To put it differently, what the agent asserts as his reason for an action must appear in a like manner to his contemporaries. Consequently, we must reconstruct the life-world of the agent and see his actions not merely as performances but as expressions of that world-view.

Thus, when we say that these modes of explanation are so many ways of answering the same question, we often misconstrue and misapprehend their nature. Besides, we reinforce the belief that these modes of explanation are comparable, and we can choose between them; we can take sides and unequivocally assert that a particular method is best suited for the social sciences. The contest between these modes of inquiry has been carried on for a considerable length of time. Philosophers of social science have, time and again, privileged one method or another on the ground that it is best suited for analysing the object of social sciences. While this has led to the redefinition of causation and sometimes even the displacement of causal explanations, nevertheless, the belief that the nature of the object of social sciences warrants a particular mode of inquiry requires closer scrutiny. There are undoubtedly significant differences between the object of analysis in the natural sciences and the social sciences but it is debatable whether the object is conceived of in the same way in the different disciplines of the social sciences—indeed, whether it is conceived of in the same way even within the boundaries of a particular discipline. While emphasizing the differences between the natural sciences and the social sciences, we can unhesitatingly assert that the latter deal with objects that are the creations of the human spirit. Yet the manner in which the sociologist and the historian, or even different sociologists, apprehend and analyse the same constructed object varies quite significantly. For instance, in a study on crime and violence, a sociologist may explore the relationship between incidents of violence, population density and poverty: he may examine if there is a positive correlation between each of these variables. Another sociologist may, on the other hand, relate the form that violence takes in the rural and urban areas to the notions of self and other in those communities. Thus, some sociologists may see violence as a phenomenon in the external world that can be counted, measured, quantified and related to other material processes in society; others may see it as an expression that manifests the values and life-world of a group of people. Accordingly, one may explain the frequency of such events by referring to observable and quantifiable social and economic factors, while another may construct the notion of self, other and criminality for a given community of people. Thus, the object of analysis may be constituted differently even within the boundaries of a particular discipline, and a correspondingly different method can be applied for studying it.

Consequently, if we privilege any one method in absolute terms we would have to privilege a particular conception of the object of social analysis. On considering the history of the social sciences and the dominant biases, indeed one is inclined to privilege the hermeneutic perception and to emphasize those methods that see the object as an expression and a structure of signification. But what is historically necessary can be privileged only contingently and not absolutely. In other words, it cannot be the basis of claiming unconditionally that this is the only reliable and adequate way of studying the social sciences. In any case, if we were to consider interpretive inquiry as the only legitimate kind of social science then we would need to radically alter the existing boundaries of disciplines. But, more importantly, we would weaken these disciplines. Analysis of correlations among different variables and the study of the functions of structures can, in many ways, supplement and strengthen particular narratives; they can, on occasion, even serve a practical interest. For instance, a study that establishes a positive relationship between violence and the erosion of traditional loyalties can supplement the narratives of industrializing societies. Indeed, it can be used to argue that the increase in violence cannot be treated merely as a law and order problem. It must be related to the inability of modern society to provide an alternative basis of identification. This itself can help us to understand the agent's world-view, to see that his existing perceptions and beliefs point to the fragmentation of his world-view. Given these possibilities, we must be extremely cautious about banishing causal analyses from the domain of the social sciences. What we need to do instead is to scrutinize our received conceptions of method and scientificity, and to recognize the implications of the way we apprehend and analyse the object.

Accordingly, the preceding discussion on the different modes of inquiry must not be seen as an attempt to privilege any one method absolutely and unconditionally. The discussion of particular modes of inquiry must be placed in the context of the specific conceptions of the nature of social science and judged in terms of what they seek to analyse and what they exclude from examination. The causal mode of explanation appears to be inadequate only on these grounds. If we cannot even identify a condition that is contingently necessary in the social world, then the use of causal language seems redundant. Further, if most events in this field are ovedetermined then we need a form of explanation that can dispense with the language of necessity that is central to the discourse on causal explanations. Reason-action explanations certainly offer an alternative to the causal mode of explanation but they only explain actions of individuals, and account for an event only to the extent that it is a consequence of any of those actions. Relatively speaking, the narrative appears to be more suitable for explaining an event in its specificity. The hermeneutic method embodies a conception of historicality that must inform all analyses, however, it presents events only from the agent's point of view. Unlike reason-action explanations, it places before us the agent's world-view, and this acquaintance with the other widens our horizon and often reveals the limitations of our own world-view. In this way, hermeneutic accounts serve a practical and critical function; in fact, to challenge the hegemony of the dominant groups, historians sometimes construct the chain of events in the voice of those agents and groups which had been marginalized in earlier narratives. However, such accounts must be differentiated from the narrative mode of inquiry where the sequence of events and actions is constructed by the historian on the basis of documents that record the voices of different agents, so that the account of events in one can be corroborated by the other. This difference is significant because the authenticity of the material used for constructing the situation and the actions of individuals determine, to a considerable extent, the adequacy of this historical account. The hermeneutic mode of inquiry enables us to understand the other, to make sense of its cultural and social practices, but, to explain the changes in these practices and to relate them to other spheres of societal organization, we need to rely on other modes of inquiry. The narrative is efficacious for it can supplement the hermeneutic account and explain the occurrence of an event, while also embodying the historical consciousness that forms the core of the hermeneutic mode of understanding.

Besides, the narrative mode bridges the distance between *Verstehen* and *Erklärer*, and challenges many of the established dichotomies of philosophic discourse. If the advocates of causal explanation drew a line between knower and known, subject and object, structure and agency, external conditions and intentionality, determination and volition, description and explanation, Dilthey also reaffirmed the dichotomy between understanding and explanation, reader and author, subjective and objective analysis. Although he changed the meaning and content of several of these categories, he defined the process of knowledge in the same mutually exclusive categories. He assumed that the meaning of a text is created by the author: it is something that is contained in the text. And the task of the reader

/analyst is to recover the meaning that the contemporaries of the author would have recovered from the text. In other words, he wanted the analyst to recover the meaning that is already present in the text, without bringing to bear upon it the biases of his historical vision. Thus he retained the distinction between the subject and the object, the historian and the text. The strength of the narrative is that it transcends these dichotomies. Instead of postulating a firm opposition, it envisages an ongoing communication between the two categories in many of these dichotomies. For instance, it weaves together the disparate elements of structure and agency, determination and intentionality to explain what happened, how it happened and why it happened. At the same time, it recognizes and affirms the interpretive nature of historical inquiry and suggests that each presentation of the past involves a re-figuration of the pre-figured world. The re-figuration, however, is neither arbitrary nor subjective. The pattern of concrete relationships and interactions is drawn on the basis of available records and survivals. Hence, it can be challenged on the basis of its analysis of different structures, its account of the actions of individual agents and presentation of the sequence of events.

This does not, however, imply that all history is, or must necessarily be, narrative in structure. Several historical accounts merely delineate the nature of prevalent structures; yet others paint a picture of the 'spirit of the age'. Each of them represents a legitimate and important account of a specific historical time. Only when we try to explain the occurrence of a determinate historical event, the narrative mode appears, in many ways, to be more adequate than causal explanation. The latter is a deterministic and reductionist form of explanation. By emphasizing external conditions and determination by structures (even though these are, in the ultimate analysis, constituted by men), causal explanations negate the subject. By referring actively to the intentions, decisions and actions of determinate agents, the narrative rescues the subject and places him in the foreground of the historical process. Further, it presents the subject as a determinate historical being, not as the abstract attributeless self of liberal discourse nor as the neutral and interchangeable entity of scientistic discourse, but as a member of a determinate group possessing and reflecting the beliefs and perceptions of that community.

Understood in this way, the narrative is essentially a signifier of a new type of politics and a protest against the dominant rationality of the Enlightenment. In place of a single pattern of individual, social and historical development, it stresses difference: indeed, it celebrates difference. And it is this celebration that finds an expression in its emphasis on the study of history and its conception of historical events as unique particulars. The belief that historical events are unique occurrences further challenges the enlightenment view that we can learn lessons from our past. The narrativists, however, maintain that the study of history serves a practical interest. It presents the richness and diversity of human experience and life, and places before us different aspects of ourselves. Displacing notions of an intrinsic and essential nature of man, it offers the only possible way by which we can know anything about human beings: their specific endeavours, beliefs and patterns of life. And this record of determinate projects presents alternatives to our contemporary way of life and modes of action and organization, which we may or may not accept. Nevertheless, it has the possibility of serving a critical interest. Besides, its emphasis on the specificity of an event marks the end of the era of metanarratives. Presenting a narrative of particular events, groups and communities, and bringing into social discourse voices that had often been suppressed or marginalized, it has helped to empower these groups and place them in the mainstream of political life.

As we privilege the narrative contingently, we must take cognizance of these political implications and place them along with other methodological considerations because only then can we comprehend the historical prejudice in favour of the narrative, and recognize that the construction of different narratives is, in many ways, reflective of the contest of power in a society which cannot be settled on purely methodological grounds. The absence of a methodological criterion does not, however, imply that all accounts are equally valid and reliable. Every historical narrative, as argued earlier, is subject to close scrutiny; its analysis of different structures and its delineation of the historical situation and actions of agents can be challenged on grounds of accuracy, detail and comprehensiveness. Hence one can distinguish an adequate narrative from an inaccurate and unreliable one. However, convincing and adequate accounts of events written from the point of view of specific groups—e.g., women and peasants—can be placed beside one another, not because they supplement each other but because they reveal the complexity of our historical being and disclose the limitations of each account. Since there is no theoretical grid from which we can view the world in itself and write its history, we must allow points of view that offer new insights and uncover different aspects of reality some space to exist.

VI

Epilogue: Postmodern Anti-Foundationalism

The most striking intellectual development of the 1980s was the ascendance of postmodernism. At a time when all other theoretical systems were retreating somewhat shamefacedly, postmodernism came up from behind to fill in the intellectual void. What attracted social scientists to postmodernism was its denunciation of metanarratives, foundationalism and essentialism. Going against the received epistemologies, postmodernism challenged the goal of producing universal knowledge and searching for determinate structural identities. Its conceptions were, in this sense, a departure from our ingrained habits of looking for deep meanings and structures in what is the ephemeral present. While this perspective on anti-foundationalism was avowedly a critique of the grand explanatory theories, postmodernism, it must be noted, was not devoid of its own brand of high theory. It had an agenda of its own and offered a distinct conception of what is the 'social' and how it can be approached and analysed. As such it contained both an epistemological and ontological orientation; and what is perhaps equally important, this orientation was sharply different from hermeneutic conceptions of plurality and heterogeneity.

Although postmodernism has been described both as a historical condition[1] and a stage of social-economic development,[2] it derives its

[1] See, F. Lyotard, *The Postmodern Condition: A Report on Knowledge*, trans. by G. Bennington and B. Massumi, Manchester University Press, Manchester, 1987.
[2] David Harvey describes postmodernism as the culture of late/post-Fordist capitalism, and Frederic Jameson too associates it with a distinct form of economic

staying power from the anti-foundational philosophies of Jacques Derrida, Richard Rorty and Gilles Deluze. In fact, the attributes of the postmodern condition along with the concepts associated with it, are identical to or supportive of the philosophical values stressed by the anti-foundational agenda. For instance, Harvey's reference to the relative insignificance of class conflict in western societies and the primacy accorded to exchange over production relations, reinforces the theoretical critiques of Marxism as a 'metanarrative'. References to the emergence of new class alliances and antagonisms support the anti-foundationalist disbelief in a single project of human emancipation. On the one hand, it questions the designation of the working class as the revolutionary subject of history, and, on the other, it reinforces belief in plural projects of emancipation. Similarly, the slogan, 'think globally, act locally', characteristic of the postmodern condition, echoes the philosophic emphasis on 'local determinism' and local management;[3] and the eclectic pursuit of diverse tastes foregrounds diversity, difference and fragmentation. Thus, even though the analysts of the postmodern condition point to the emergence of a new set of cultural and aesthetic norms, their analyses offer a methodological justification of the anti-foundational philosophical agenda. Hence, the two representations of postmodernism have complemented each other. Collectively they have effected a profound change in the intellectual mood and language of academic discourse. Indeed they have created an environment in which rationalist beliefs that characterised scientific enquiry since the time of Plato, are being questioned and undermined.

II

The Postmodern intellectual agenda is constituted by two distinct moments: a) of negation, wherein the search for foundations is

organization. Both relate postmodernism with specific social and economic structures and a distinct stage of historical development. F. Jameson, *Postmodernism, or, the Cultural Logic of Late Capitalism*, Verso, London, 1991; and D. Harvey, *The Condition of Postmodernity*, Basil Blackwell, Oxford, 1989.

[3] J.F. Lyotard, *The Postmodern Condition: A Report on Knowledge*, trans. by G. Bennington and B. Massumi, Manchester University Press, Manchester, 1987, p. xxiv.

criticised; and b) of affirmation, where its own anti-foundational language is enunciated. The latter is, to a considerable extent, predicated on the former. In fact it offers an alternative to foundational languages. However, to grasp the meaning and implication of this anti-foundational language, it is necessary to begin with the postmodern understanding of foundationalism.

For the postmodernists, Foundationalism represents the search for an absolute and unconditional ground on which existence can be predicated and universal knowledge claims asserted. Judging by this criterion, traditional metaphysics and epistemology epitomize foundationalism. The former postulates God as the ultimate ground of all existence and then tries to unveil or discover the presence of this fundamental Being in all beings. It is thus engaged in the determination of Being as *presence* in all senses of the word. Pointing to this aspect of metaphysics, Derrida argues that, '[I]t would be possible to show that all the names related to fundamentals, to principles, or to the center have always designated the constant of a presence — *eidos, arche, telos, energeia, ousia* (essence, existence, substance, subject) *aletheia*, transcendentality, consciousness, or conscience, God men and so forth'.[4]

If metaphysics is obsessed with the idea of Being as presence, epistemology too is permeated by the same concern. To this end it employs the notion of absolute truth and tries to identify the ground on which truth claims can be asserted and arguments conclusively won. Further, it endeavours to determine a universal criterion on the basis of which a vocabulary can be privileged or displaced.

According to the postmodernists, the foundationalist projects of traditional metaphysics and epistemology are shared by philosophy in general. Philosophy, with its emphasis on absolute universals and theory, is quintessentially foundationalist. However, it is not the only form of enquiry that manifests a foundationalist bias. From the postmodernist perspective, science too is a foundational enterprise. Although science questions the notion of an Absolute God, the transcendental is manifested in the scientific secular world in the form of a rational plans, or laws, of nature and history. Moreover, scientific

---

[4] Derrida quoted in G. Spivak, 'Introduction' to J. Derrida, *Of Grammatology*, trans. by G. Spivak, The John Hopkins University Press, Baltimore, Maryland, 1976, p. xxi.

theories also attempt to present a 'mirror image' of the external world: like philosophy they claim to discover the truth, or more appropriately, the *essential* nature of reality. Thus, despite the difference in their respective orientations, postmodernism maintains that both philosophy and science are similar kinds of enquiry as they are equally committed to the search for foundations, or essences, of entities. Further, the postmodernists argue that this search assumes, quite uncritically, that there is a super-vocabulary in which the essential and necessary attributes of an entity can be captured and represented.

To put it differently, both philosophy and science postulate the existence of absolute, unified, coherent entities, such as, nature, history, society and the human self. Both assume that we can recover the essence of these entities without problematizing the nature of linguistic mediation. The only significant difference between them being that philosophy sees reason as the mode of arriving at that self identical truth, while science proceeds through systematic observation and generalization. In each case language is taken to be a self evident medium of representation, calmly mirroring the world outside. Expressing deep skepticism of such a naive view of language, postmodernists insist that questions of the following kind must be raised: 'Is the language we are presently using the "right" language — is it adequate to its task as a medium of expression or representation?' Such questions assume that there are relations such as 'fitting the world' or 'being faithful to the true nature of the self....'[5] What unites philosophy and science then is the belief that there are non-linguistic things called 'meanings' or 'facts', and the task of language is to represent them faithfully and accurately. To this end, philosophy frequently assumes a one-to-one relationship between the signifier and the signified, and science presupposes a theory independent, neutral observation language. Both believe that the aim of systematic enquiry is to grasp the essence of an entity, or what amounts to the same thing, its 'necessary attributes'.[6] The entity in question may be the human self, nature, history or society; each is said to have an

[5] R. Rorty, 'The Contingency of Language', *London Review of Books*, 17 April, 1986(a).

[6] E. Laclau, *New Reflections on the Revolution of our Time*, Verso, London, 1990, p. 114.

intrinsic nature which the analyst must seek to discover, or more appropriately, uncover. The alliance between philosophy and science on this count is significant for the postmodernists because both are paradigmatic human activities, and interestingly enough, they prescribe the same conception of truth, knowledge and science. Both presuppose the existence of essences, and consequently, of universal and unconditional ground. Foundationalism or essentialism is thus their common legacy.

The Enlightenment rationality too was an expression of this foundationalist perspective. It recommended the search for invariable laws of history,[7] and its narratives about the 'activities of such entities as the monumental self, or the Absolute Spirit or the Proletariat' were all enterprises inspired by foundationalism.[8] Quite plainly, from the antifoundational perspective of postmodernism, the Enlightenment and its many projects were deeply flawed. The grand explanatory schemas, or metanarratives, that sought to describe and predict the movement of such entities as the working class, the rational subject, wealth, Spirit or history, suffered from a variety of methodological lacunae. a) These metanarratives had been falsified empirically. b) They imbued each entity with an intrinsic nature, that was there to be 'discovered' by human beings, not 'made' or 'created' by them. Since the intrinsic nature or essence was there, existing quite independent of the agents, these metanarratives focussed on structure rather than agency; they analysed the laws of historical development, and relatively speaking, neglected the study of consciousness. c) The metanarratives of the Enlightenment also obscured the particular in history. In the words of Lyotard, metanarratives, unlike little stories, do not receive or bestow names. For instance, 'the great story of history has its end in the extinction of names (particularisms). At the end of the great story there will simply be humanity. The names humanity has taken will turn out to be superfluous, at best they will have designated certain stations along the way to the cross'.[9] d) Metanarratives tend to reduce the

[7] See, H.T. Buckle, *Civilization in England*, vol. I, Watts & Co., London, 1930; and J.B. Bury, 'The Science of History', in F. Stern (ed.), *The Varieties of History from Voltaire to the Present*, Thames and Hudson, London, 1970.

[8] R. Rorty, *Philosophy and the Mirror of Nature*, Basil Blackwell, Oxford, 1980, p. 585; and Lyotard, 1987, op. cit., p. xxiii.

[9] J.F. Lyotard, *The Differend: Phases in Dispute*, trans. by G. Van der Abbele,

plurality of social processes to the working of a dominant structure or identity. That is, the historical process is analysed and explained in terms of an identifiable dominant structure. It is seen as the necessary outcome of this primary structure. By arguing that the event is determined by the primary structure, and within marxism by the primary contradiction, such analyses place a 'closure' upon the historical process and severely constrain freedom.[10]

The grand narratives of the Enlightenment rested on the mistaken belief that history, society, the human self and God, have an *intrinsic* nature and an identifiable, *coherent* essence. The postmodernists question this understanding and argue that there is no such thing as *intrinsic* nature, an *objective* reality or an accurate *representation* of the world as it is in itself. Just as there are no universal laws of history operating independently of particular agents, similarly, there is no truth out there, existing independently of the human mind, waiting to be 'discovered'.[11] In place of the enlightenment's faith in science and technological success, postmodernism asserts that science is just another human activity comparable to literature and politics. To quote Rorty, 'Great scientists *invent* descriptions of the world which are useful for purposes of predicting and controlling what happens, just as poets and political theorists invent other descriptions of it for other purposes.'[12] The idea that there is some truth that can be discovered by scientific observation or philosophic reason was, for the postmodernists, a legacy of an age in which the world was seen as the creation of a Being who had a language of Her own. It assumes the existence of a 'super vocabulary' through which the divine project can be described and represented. For the advocates of postmodernism, both these ideas stemmed from the fundamental belief that there are non-linguistic things called 'meanings' and 'essences', and the task of language is to express these meanings and represent these essences. Above all else, the postmodernists question this conception of language. We must, they argue, drop the idea that language is a *system of representation*.

Arguing against the language of representation, mirroring and

University of Minnesota Press, Minneapolis, 1988, p. 155.

[10] E. Laclau, op. cit., p. 50.

[11] R. Rorty, 1986 (a), op. cit.

[12] Ibid., p. 3, emphasis added.

correspondence, the postmodernists maintain that it is no longer appropriate to speak of a language as being adequate or inadequate representation of the world or the self. All languages are human constructs and they mediate our descriptions of the world. In other words, what we have are *descriptions*, not representations or mirror images of the world. Further, these descriptions are communicated linguistically. Hence, we see the world as it appears to us through the limits that are inherent in our language or conceptual grid. More importantly, since we only have descriptions of the world, we can speak merely of the truth or falsehood of these descriptions. As such, truth is a property of linguistic entities. It does not refer to an accurate representation of the world in itself.

Further, as all claims about the nature of the world are embodied in language and mediated through our theoretical paradigm, we never know the world in itself. What we see and know is the world as it appears to us through the lens of our paradigm. Our descriptions of the world are not therefore mirror images of the world outside. Instead they are human constructs, devised, used and judged by their capacity to perform certain tasks. It is therefore important to reflect upon the language-game in which sentences are formulated and represent-ations encoded. Moreover, since language does not provide a mirror image of the world outside, what we can do is to examine the way in which the self is constituted in each vocabulary and language game.

Quite obviously, the world does not propose a language for us, and it does not also tell us what language-game to play. Conse-quently, there are no 'foundations' or 'universal rules' that can serve as common ground for adjudicating between diverse knowledge claims and descriptions of the world.[13] In other words, change from one language game to another cannot be explained by any one criterion: 'a universal rule of judgement between heterogeneous games is lacking in general'.[14] In fact, the postmodernists maintain that the search for such a universal criterion is rooted in a foun-dationalist world view, hence, we must resist the temptation to look for a single principle on the basis of which changes in vocabularies can be explained and arguments decisively concluded.

[13] R. Rorty, 1980, op. cit., p. 317; and J.F. Lyotard, 1988, op. cit., p. xi.
[14] J.F. Lyotard, ibid.

While questioning the possibility of knowing the world in itself, the advocates of postmodernism do not redefine or historicise the notion of truth. Instead they feel that to talk of the nature of truth, like that of God or self, is an unprofitable subject. What we need to remember is that there are no absolute referents in the form of 'intrinsic nature' or 'pure essence', and there is no sacred meaning that can give direction to our deeds. Meaning is an object of self creation: it is to be made, not discovered.[15]

Postmodernism presents this view of the world and the cognitive process as a refutation of the empiricist conception of science and the enlightenment's quest for philosophic or scientific certitude. Through it the advocates of postmodernism question the belief that there is a world out there, existing independently of the knower, which is accessible to us through sensory perception, and made available to us by science. To put it a little differently, postmodernism challenges the idea of representation embodied in the correspondence theory of truth. Like other critics of the causal model, it maintains that explaining events by subsuming them under a general law is inadequate and reductionist. However, unlike them, it does not advocate the study of reasons, intentions or historical contexts. Indeed it remains critical of narrative constructions, genealogies and all other attempts to reconstruct meanings of texts. Against all these forms of understanding, it celebrates difference and emphasises the need to deconstruct, discover and invent meanings. This gives a new and positive content to the postmodern intellectual agenda.

III

In a way postmodern anti-foundationalism is the 'other' of foundationalism. If foundationalism is the language associated with essence, presence, transparency of meaning, representation, determination, and a coherent, unified and single truth, then postmodern anti-foundationalism refers to absent presence, trace, *differance*, ambiguity, non-determination, plurality, incoherence and inconsistency of meanings. What is perhaps equally important is that the concepts which

[15] R. Rorty, 'The Contingency of Selfhood', *London Review of Books*, 8 May, 1986(b). Also see, R. Rorty 1986(a), op. cit.

express the anti-foundational agenda affirm the view that texts are multivocal and their meaning cannot be restricted to any single referent. Indeed the meaning of the text must be continuously deconstructed and created anew.

For the postmodernists meaning can be created because there is no transcendental signified and, therefore, no absolute or pre-given meaning. But even more significantly because the signifier and the signified are separated from each other; there is a 'distance', a 'space' between them.[16] Although the postmodernists accept that the signifier can signify only if it bears some relation to the signified, yet, from their perspective, the important thing is that the signifier is characterized by a 'surplus'. That is, it supplements the thing itself.[17] It neither exhausts nor is exhausted by the signified. Since the sign is not a representation or a copy of the signified, it cannot be reduced to a single identifiable object or meaning. All we can say about the sign as a text is that it resonates with several meaning. Like any form of 'gramme' (graphe or writing), it transcends its author and the point of its origin.[18] Just as writing, even in the limited sense of an inscription, 'carries with it a force of breaking with its context, that is, the set of presences which organize the moment of its inscription',[19] similarly, the sign marks the

[16] J. Derrida, *Of Grammatology*, trans. by G.C. Spivak, The John Hopkins University Press, Baltimore, Maryland, 1976, pp. 68–9; and J. Derrida, *Margins of Philosophy*, trans. by Alan Bass, Chicago University Press, Chicago, p. 9.

[17] J. Derrida, 1976, op. cit., pp. 144–5.

[18] J. Derrida, 1982, op. cit., p. 317. Derrida uses the notion of *arche* writing to elucidate the idea of anti-foundationalism, and, conversely, he associates the primacy ordinarily accorded to speech with the prevalence of the metaphysics of presence. Consequently, by 'deconstructing the privilege of the spoken word' (Spivak 1976: Li) and recognising the presence of writing in speech, he attempts to question the metaphysics of presence (Derrida 1982: 291). Derrida writes, 'We already have a foreboding that phonocentricism merges with the historical determination of the meaning of being in general as *presence*, with all the subdeterminations which depend on this general form and which organise within it their system and their historical sequence (presence of the thing to the sight as *eidos*, presence as substance/ essence/ existence [*ousia*], temporal presence as point [*stigme*] of the now or of the moment [*nun*], the self presence of the cogito, consciousness, subjectivity, the co-presence of the other and of the self . . . and so forth' (Derrida 1976: 12).

[19] J. Derrida, 1982, op. cit., p. 317.

distance between the signifier and the signified. In other words its meaning is not exhausted by the author's intentions or the particularity of the historical context.

Derrida uses the example of writing to elucidate the notion of anti-foundationalism because it represents a form of distantiation. Unlike the spoken word, a written text is available to every one who knows that language. Hence, it is open to diverse interpretations. To put it in another way, the written text distances itself from the author, the original context and its addressees. As it is read in different contexts and from different perspectives, it is open to new readings and meanings. The point that needs to be emphasised in this connection is that hermeneutic enquiry assumes that the purpose of understanding is to *recover* the meaning that the text had for its original addressee. For this reason, the hermeneuticians try to reconstruct the original historical context through systematic exegesis. The postmodernists, by comparison, want to liberate the text from its historical context, author and his original addressees. Further, unlike hermeneutic understanding, postmodernism does not locate plural readings in the diversity of historical worlds of the readers. For the postmodernists, multivocality of texts or the plurality of meanings is not an attribute of the historicity of the reader. It is instead the hallmark of all texts, or all writing in general. Since the graphic sign always 'stands for something which is missing, always substitutes itself for the immediate presence of a thing, always shows itself in the stead of the thing itself',[20] it resonates with many meanings. It is, in other words, multivocal.

Postmodernism suggests that the reader or the analyst must approach the text with this awareness of the 'arbitrariness' of the sign and the indeterminacy of meaning. This implies that the search for a unified coherent meaning within the text must be given up.[21] In fact, we should not see the text as a unified single whole. Instead of weaving the different parts of the text into a single coherent meaning or central argument, the focus should be on the inconsistencies and the contradictions of meaning in the text. In other words, in place of harmonizing the

[20] E.T. Bannet, *Structuralism and the Logic of Dissent*, Methuen, London, 1989, p. 191.

[21] As Laclau would say, texts are always 'incoherent', 'ambiguous' and 'inherently incomplete' (Laclau 1990, op. cit., pp. 28–9).

apparent contradictions and bringing out the essential meaning of the text, reading should draw upon the inconsistencies and obscurities inherent in the text and point to the presence of plural and diverse voices within the text.

To discover the multivocality of the text, the postmodernists claim that the word be read as a trace of all its possible meanings that lie within the text and also outside of it. That is, instead of restricting the meaning of a word to its particular usage in a context, postmodernists suggest that we supplement it with other meanings that the word has in other passages of the text and those that it has outside the text. To this end, in his own reading, Derrida hyphenated words — for instance, 'no-thing', 'de-limitation', 'ek-sist'[22] to conjure new images and to draw out meanings that may have been suppressed or lost in a particular context. Elsewhere, he refers to other words with which a given word shares a phonic similarity or a common linguistic root — e.g., *different*, and *differends, marge-marque-marche*[23] — with a view, once again, to dissolving the boundaries of the text. Just as he introduces other texts in his reading of a given text, he also questions, and sometimes reverses, existing hierarchies by making the minor term in paired opposites as the ground and condition for the existence of that which is customarily seen to be the major term. Thus, for instance, he challenges and displaces the prominence hitherto accorded to speech *vis-à-vis* writing, presence *vis-à-vis* absence, centre *vis-à-vis* margins. Rupturing the unity of the text, dividing it against itself and inscribing or grafting new meanings into it, are, in this framework, strategies aimed at *deconstructing* the text. They seek to interrogate the supposed truth content of the text and the certitude of our inherited conceptions. By linking meanings present in the text with those that are absent but can nevertheless be traced to it, the postmodernists question, reverse, or displace existing hierarchies and insert, what Derrida calls, the 'critical text' into the reading.

Reading absences and inserting new meanings are strategies employed by postmodernism to deconstruct the text and open it to meanings that had not been intended by the author or recovered in the original context. In fact these means are employed to affirm the view

[22] J. Derrida, 1982, op. cit., pp. 39, 60 and 129 respectively.
[23] Ibid., pp. 8 and 12 respectively.

that knowledge is not a system of 'tracking down' or 'discovering' truth. It is, instead, the field of 'freeplay . . . a field of infinite substitutions in the closure of a finite ensemble'.[24] In other words, these are modes of deconstructing a text and transcending the conceptual closure imposed by the metaphysics of presence. They make texts multivocal, and this multivocality reminds us that no matter how hard we try, our reading will always remain incomplete. There will always be an 'otherness' — a residual content — that escapes and cannot be appropriated by us.

Postmodern anti-foundationalism, in this way, creates space for dissonance and difference. It acknowledges the presence of the 'other' within the boundaries of the self. The epistemological space provided for the 'other' in the postmodern project has come to symbolize a political and philosophical perspective in which freedom, diversity and plurality are the core norms.[25] Translated in this form, the postmodernist perspective has been used to question social, cultural and national norms. In western societies the postmodernism has challenged the logos of the white man and attempted to create space for the 'other' in it. It has, in this connection, lent support to the new social movements, particularly for the demand to protect and ensure diversity of values and lifestyles. Against the Eurocentric perspective of the Enlightenment, postmodernism has drawn attention to the ethnic and the oriental. In fact, it makes 'ethnos' an authentic and primary category of social analysis and legitimizes the belief that 'groups have a right to speak for themselves and in their own voices'.[26] In these and other associated ways, postmodernism has come to represent an attitude of tolerance and respect for the other. On the one hand, it assumes that '[I]t is precisely in loosing the certainty of truth and the unanimous agreement of others that man becomes an individual',[27] and on the other, it upholds values through which 'individuals and communities

[24] J. Derrida, 1976, op. cit., p. 51.
[25] 'The Irreductibility of the Spacing', wrote Derrida, 'is the irreductibility of the other' (Quoted in Bannet 1989, op. cit., p. 223).
[26] D. Harvey, 1989, op. cit., p. 48.
[27] R. Rorty, 'Philosophers, Novelists and Inter-cultural Comparisons: Heidegger, Kundera and Dickens', paper presented at the 6th East-West Philosophers Conference, Honolulu, July 31–Aug 11, 1989, p. 18.

could coexist peacefully with other individuals and communities' while also putting together 'new syncretic, compromise ways of life'.[28]

Although the postmodern anti-foundationalism has most often been associated with tolerance, it is necessary to iterate that this agenda also expresses the limits of human finitude. At the epistemological plane, postmodernism reveals the incompleteness of our reading and knowledge, and at the political plane, it expresses doubt in the human ability to shape the present and the future. Its adherents speak variously of powerlessness, disintegration and absolute contingency as the human predicaments. Richard Rorty refers to the self as a 'centreless, random assemblage of contingent and idiosyncratic needs';[29] a few others celebrate the absence of narrative continuity and the presence of a condition that is best described as schizophrenia. However, what is significant is that the recognition of a centreless self does not induce in the postmodernists a sense of despair or pessimism. Indeed almost all of them place a positive value on fragmentation. Lyotard maintains that a framework in which incoherence and ambiguity are positive values, will herald a complete rejection of the totalizing discourses of the nineteenth and the twentieth centuries. It will assist in waging a 'war against totality' and the associated 'nostalgia for the whole'.[30] Against the Habermasian quest for a perfect 'dialogical' society, Lyotard uses the postmodern agenda to reveal the repressive nature of the ideal of consensus (homologia). He maintains that ideals that favour 'argumentation with a view only to consensus; the unicity of the referent as a guarantee for the possibility of agreement; parity between partners; and even an indirect recognition that it is a question of a game and not a destiny . . .'[31] are new enunciations of the 'terrorist ideals of consensus'. Hence, they need to be opposed firmly.

From the postmodernist perspective, the ideology of self creation and difference offers an alternative to the existing modes of oppression and domination. The emphasis on locality, practical knowledge and

[28] R. Rorty, 'A Pragmatist View of Rationality and Cultural Difference', paper presented in Delhi, 26 December 1990, p. 1.

[29] R. Rorty quoted in N. O'Sullivan, 'Political Interrogation, the Limited State and the Philosophy of Postmodernism', in *Political Studies*, XLI, 1998, p. 30.

[30] J.F. Lyotard, 1987, op. cit., pp. 81–2.

[31] Ibid., p. 28.

political foundationalism is an expression of its rejection of scientism, bureaucratic centralism, instrumental rationality and philosophical foundationalism. Since postmodernism challenges the search for certain indubitable and foundational premises about human nature and self, it also questions the existing justifications of democracy. In fact Rorty claims that we can only offer 'apologetics', not 'justification' for our social and political choices.[32] In defence of liberal democracy we can offer arguments that make our choices comprehensible but not an argument that can settle all disputes and differences conclusively. Our choices and political preferences have to be argued for; we have to recognize their relative validity, and yet, stand up for them unflinchingly. We must be equally prepared to 'call true whatever the upshot of such encounters turns out to be'.[33] In other words, whatever be the outcome of political contestations and ideological battles, they should be accepted as the relative truth for that society. In the absence of philosophical justifications, solidarity among the members in a society cannot be assumed. It has to be expressed and continuously renewed. What is even more likely is that, on most occasions, solidarity will have to be forged among the members of a group who share a set of commitments and political-social preferences. Since there are bound to be differences among members of a society on this issue, postmodernists suggests that we need a form of 'civil association' (i.e. *societas* as opposed to *universitas*) which allows these differences to be expressed and respected.[34]

As we observed earlier, arguments about the absence of absolute justifications are used by postmodernists to support the diverse projects of emancipation — e.g. those expressed in the struggles of women, gays, environmentalists, blacks, immigrants, indigenous people, etc. A few adherents of this ism are optimistic that these diverse and heterogeneous projects would fit together in a kind of 'rainbow coalition', supporting each other and the cause of 'radical democracy'.[35] Others, however, endorse a weaker position: they point to the validity of

[32] R. Rorty, 'The Contingency of Community', *London Review of Books*, 24 July, 1986(c).
[33] Ibid.
[34] R. Rorty, 1980, op. cit., p. 318.
[35] E. Laclau, 1990, op. cit., p. 125.

diverse rationalities and projects. In the context of the eurocentric logos of enlightenment rationality, these theorists celebrate the ethnic and the oriental. This preference for ethnos and indigenous is manifested in every sphere of life: in architecture, for instance, ethnic designs and structures are used freely and eclectically to redefine space.

In sum, postmodernism expresses ontological and epistemological anti-foundationalism. It questions the existence of a transcendental signified, and, with it, the philosophic preoccupation with discovering truth. Emphasizing self creation and difference, it substitutes the desire for certitude and coherence with the notion of ambiguity and freeplay, and inserts the idea of an absent presence in the discourse of western metaphysics. Further, the postmodernist project includes a social and political agenda, that aims at empowering individuals as separate agents, while simultaneously challenging the existing modes of marginalization and domination.

IV

Postmodernism offered a systematic critique of the enlightenment rationality. However, it was not the first to embark on this course. Prior to postmodernism, historicism, hermeneutics, romanticism, critical theory and post-empiricist theories of science, had all challenged aspects of enlightenment thought. In fact, on closer scrutiny it is evident that postmodernism endorsed these critiques, but in delineating its own anti-foundational language it also questioned the assumptions of these alternative modes of enquiry. In some cases it placed these schools of thought alongside the Enlightenment and subjected them to the same critical scrutiny.

The Enlightenment continued the post-renaissance struggle for the secularisation of the social by using reason and science as its allies. The latter were the instruments with which the Enlightenment sought to dismantle what it considered to be the 'illusory', 'metaphysical' and 'false' nature of traditional religious orthodoxies and beliefs. In more positive terms, both reason and science were used to furnish a rational view of the world, human history and the self: a view which supported and furthered the ability of individuals to control and manipulate their environment so as to pave the way for a 'good' and 'rational' society.

Some of the categories of Enlightenment thought, expressed in the writings of the English and the French theorists, were questioned in the mid-eighteenth century by the German historians and philosophers. While many of them challenged the centrality given to reason by arguing that 'will', not reason, was the motive force of history, others redefined the concept of reason. Instead of positing a dichotomy between reason and tradition, they argued that reason was not an innate quality of the human mind. It was a product of development, tempered by tradition and nourished by the human will. More importantly, these German historians questioned the enlightenment belief in a single pattern of national and individual growth. Industrialization and democracy were the twin norms in terms of which the enlightenment had made a distinction between the dark ages and the brighter, enlightened present, and further, between the advanced English and French society and the 'sick', 'backward' German society. The German historians questioned this characterization of their society. Analysing the reasons for their present predicament, they argued that the history of humankind presented a succession of heterogeneous cultures, each complete in itself with its own set of values and cherished goods.[36] Diverse societies and cultures were, in other words, incommensurable and no single criterion, particularly one borrowed from our present stage of development, could be a valid basis for judging these diverse cultures.[37] To put it differently, the previous cultures could not be seen as a stepping stone for the evolution of the present; nor could the latter be a privileged vantage point for judging the past. Each social-cultural way of life had to be understood in terms of the values internal to it. To this end, Herder suggested that historians study the culture from the 'inside', by re-constructing its various aspects of life. Setting the trail for others, he in fact collected the myths, folk lore and literature of the people of the highlands who were still dominated by the medieval traditions and forms of life. Thus, Herder in association with other historians, questioned the enlightenment reading of history and its arrogant dismissal of previous ways of life as

[36] J.G. Von Herder, *On Social and Political Culture*, trans. by F.M. Barnard, Cambridge University Press, Cambridge, 1969, p. 188.

[37] Ibid., p. 231.

barbaric or primitive. In its place, they offered and cherished the ideal of diversity and irreconcilable heterogeneity. Almost a century and a half later, this was the perspective from which social anthropologists recovered and redeemed the rationality of the colonized and tribal cultures.

The German historians also questioned the methodological orthodoxies of the enlightenment by emphasizing the distinction between the natural sciences and the human sciences. The enlightenment theorists had endorsed the empiricist conception of science and advocated the extension of the methods used in the study of the natural phenomenon — e.g. search for empirical generalizations and causal explanations — to the study of the social phenomenon. From somewhat different perspectives, Wegelin, Gatterer and Chladenius rejected these beliefs. Wegelin argued that natural sciences were concerned with immutable, transcendental principles governing the world of matter, while the historical sciences analyse the changing, semi-free products of the human spirit.[38] Similarly, Chladenius distinguished between historical and dogmatic explanations. The former, he argued, investigate both the external world and the inner world of human values, while the latter deal only with the world external to man.[39] Both these historians questioned the belief that mathematics and the natural sciences provide a universal model for scientific analysis. In its place they maintained that historical knowledge was an equally important and scientific form of enquiry, albeit dealing with a different order of reality.

Further, by referring to history rather than the human/social sciences, the German historians suggested that history, not philosophy, was the queen of human sciences; while all other disciplines deal with an aspect of human life, history dealt with women and men of all ages and all times. Subsequently, other arguments were woven into this perspective. By the end of the nineteenth century some theorists interpreted this statement to stress the study of the process of development, from its moment of origin to its present stage; others pointed to the changing nature of things, and consequently, emphasized contextualism. Hegel

[38] P.H. Reill, *The German Enlightenment and the Rise of German Historicism*, University of California Press, Berkeley, 1975, p. 119.
[39] Ibid., pp. 106–7.

went a step further. He saw history as the expression of the absolute/ transcendental behind the contingent. History, he said, gives a determinate form to the Absolute Idea and represents a mode of self understanding and self awareness.

Setting aside these differences in readings, the point to note here is that the enlightenment conception of universalism and the associated belief in a single, all-encompassing unity was displaced in the mid-eighteenth and early nineteenth century, by a more complex vision of historical diversity, heterogeneity and the presence of contingency. Romanticism, in particular, emphasized the latter. While it reversed several other cognitive preferences of the enlightenment — e.g., reason with passion and intuition, cognitive certitude with doubt, prevailing optimism with scepticism about our ability to know and master the forces of nature, and the vision of historical progress with that of moral degeneration — it pointed to the contingent and man-made/chosen contexts which determined the destiny of man. The tragedy of human life was, for them, so much greater because it was self imposed: that is, it was a consequence of our following our internal compulsions and passions. The romanticists distinguished themselves from the enlightenment. 'Philosophes' in yet another way. While the latter were engaged in uncovering the true, objective nature of external reality and the human self, romanticists celebrated nature, subjective experience, feeling and desire.

What needs to be emphasized is that neither historicism nor romanticism questioned the existence of the transcendental and the universal. They merely altered the terms of discourse by owning and sometimes privileging the contingent and the heterogeneous. Further, Herder and Dilthey historicized our perceptions. They replaced the idea of a pre-given, essential and invariable nature by an historically specific and culturally defined 'spirit' or nature. Instead of delineating a universal pattern of historical development, norms and ontological essence, they spoke of diverse patterns of growth, conceptions of self, morality and organisations of society. In other words, they historicized the notion of rationality and referred to the diversity of human projects that have unfolded in history. What is perhaps important in this connection is that while acknowledging the historical nature of the subject, they did not abandon the idea of a single, objective truth. In lieu of the Enlightenment and rationalist view of a single reality and truth, they spoke of historically specific and culturally shared conceptions of reality and truth. Accordingly they looked for the meaning that the text had in the historical context in which it originated. Hence, the advocates of hermeneutics contextualised our perceptions and understanding.

At another level, these theorists of hermeneutic understanding maintained that the social reality was, directly or indirectly, the product of human creation. Literally, it represented the objectifications of the human mind/spirit (geist). However, when social reality was taken to be a human construct, it was assumed that its distinctive cultural voice or historical spirit can be recovered. The search for an objective truth was therefore not abandoned; only the empiricist conception of objective reality and ahistorical truth was rejected. Since the historian was called upon to recover a meaning that members of a society (socio-cultural-historical entity) would have recovered from the text in accordance with the practices of shared language game, it was assumed that subsequent readings of the text would reaffirm that one and the same meaning. Hence, objectivity was not sacrificed, and disputes about the meaning of the text could in principle be settled.

In this way, hermeneutic philosophy abandoned the notion of an essential and universal truth: it historicized our conceptions of life, human self, morality and society. Further, it legitimized the different patterns of rationality articulated in diverse historical-cultural units, and gave them respect and authenticity. Since philosophy as a form of enquiry tried to overcome the sense of difference and contingency, hermeneutic inquiry relegated it to a subordinate position, giving the pride of place to history. History came to represent both a mode of knowing and a mode of being. No longer were the historians expected to penetrate the veil of being to glimpse at the universal Being that must lie behind this plurality. Instead, their ostensible task was to recover the meaning that the original addressee would have derived from the text. Hence, neither the existence of the author nor his authority were denied or questioned. It was assumed that the author was, through the text, communicating with other contemporaries and was, therefore, using language in accordance with the norms/meanings shared between her and her contemporaries (the original addressee). The task of enquiry was therefore to reconstruct that language game in which the text was encoded. In contradistinction, romanticism spoke of forging a psychological unity with the author while simultaneously recognizing the virtual impossibility of reliving the life of the 'genius' or, for that matter, the moment of creativity. Troubled by this paradox, it agonised about our ability to understand the text completely. Hermeneutic framework, on the other hand, overcame this dilemma by limiting understanding to the recovery of that meaning which the original addressee would have derived from the text. Recovering the author's original intentions or the moment of creativity was not a part of this enterprise.

Hermeneutic philosophy thus provided a critique of a historical and essentialist readings, and it also opposed what Rorty calls 'bad foundationalism'. However, it concerned itself only with those aspects of the enlightenment that applied to the human historical world; it did not, in other words, question the notion of natural science and scientific method that underpinned that thinking. The latter task was performed almost a century after by the post empiricist philosophies of science, most notably by Kuhn, Feyerabend and Putnam. Each of them emphasized the place of interpretation and theory in scientific observation and theory formation. Perhaps the weakest expression of this view was present in the writings of Popper in the form of 'Searchlight theory': that is, the statement that what we see depends to a considerable extent on what the light illuminates.[40] While our perception is also to some extent shaped by the nature of the object on which the light is focussed, the position of the subject and the nature of her concerns make a crucial difference to what is observed. Kuhn and Hanson made a stronger claim. They argued that we see the world only through some theoretical paradigm or grid. Or, to put it differently, the same visual experience may be registered variously by people possessing incommensurate theoretical paradigms. For instance, Johannes Kepler and Tycho Brahe may have had the same visual experience as they watched the sun rise but what they 'saw' while watching the dawn was quite different. While Tycho Brahe saw the sun rise, Kepler saw the earth moving so that the sun came into view.

[40] K. Popper, *The Open Society and its Enemies*, vol. I, Routledge and Kegan Paul, London, 1966, p. 260.

Seeing something is, in other words, an act of interpretation. To cite an example: seeing the figure first as an antelope and then as a pelican 'involves interpreting the lines differently in each case, then having a different interpretation of [the] figure . . . just *is* for us to see something different'.[41] Consequently, it is not as if we see the same thing and then interpret it differently: instead the data itself changes from paradigm to paradigm. What appears to a common man as a lamp bulb is to a physicist an x-ray tube; and what Tycho Brahe saw as a pipe, Kepler would have seen as a telescope, an instrument about which his friend Galileo had written to him.[42]

Post-empiricist philosophers of science argued that people with different paradigms see the world differently. It is not as if they interpret the same set of observed facts differently, but that they see quite different facts. Besides, observing something means identifying it and giving it a name.[43] And naming a thing or categorizing it involves the use of a disciplinary matrix. Consequently there is no way in which we can know the world in itself or say that the picture derived from a particular paradigm is an objective representation or a mirror image of the world outside. All knowledge, even that of the natural sciences is mediated through conceptual schemas and subject to interpretation by the members of the scientific community.[44]

Postmodernism endorsed these critiques of empiricist conception of science and it also shared the hermeneutic concern with meaning. It accepted the idea that there is no neutral and theory independent observation language: that all enquiry, including that of the natural sciences, employs a theoretical paradigm, and is subject to interpretation. Science's claim to represent pure objectivity was, therefore, a myth and the accompanying belief that scientific theories represent a

[41] N.R. Hanson quoted in Suppe, *The Structure of Scientific Theories*, University of Illinois Press, Urbana, 1977, p. 154. Also see, N.R. Hanson, 'Observation as Theory Laden', in S. Brown, J. Fauvel and R. Finnegan (eds), *Conceptions of Inquiry*, Methuen & Co. in association with Open University Press, New York, 1981, pp. 262–3.

[42] N.R. Hanson, 1981, op. cit., pp. 265–7.

[43] T. Kuhn, 'Second Thoughts on Paradigms', in F. Suppe (ed.), 1977, op. cit., pp. 463–80.

[44] N.R. Hanson, 1981, op. cit., pp. 262–7.

mirror image of the world outside, completely erroneous. However, while endorsing these perceptions, postmodernism did not begin from the point where these post-empiricist or hermeneutic theories had left off. In fact, it chose a different starting point: it opposed the metaphysics of presence itself and argued that hermeneutic philosophy shared the methodological errors of the former. Dilthey, for instance, attempted to recover from the text a meaning that was pre-given; a meaning that was placed in the text by the author. In other words, he assumed the unity of the text and the presence of a coherent meaning. He placed a closure on enquiry by stipulating that the historian should recover the meaning of the text by re-constructing the objective mind of that society — that is, the original context of experience. Postmodernism, particularly the post-structuralist component of it, questioned the assumptions of such hermeneutic analysis. It argued for the autonomy of the text, and sought to free it from the constraints placed by the author, the original context and the original addressee. It maintained that meaning is always delayed, deferred and disseminated; further, it located the possibilities of critical reading in the idea that words do not have a single determinate meaning, and like metaphors in language, they invoke diverse images and meanings that can be used to reveal aspects of the text that might be lost in earlier forms of hermeneutic reading.

Thus, postmodernism displaced the hermeneutic faith in the recovery of a single, historically and culturally specific meaning with the twin ideas of indeterminacy of meaning and absence of closure. While these ideas, like hermeneutic philosophy and post-empiricist conceptions of science, offered a critique of the Enlightenment conception of history and science, they conceived the task of the human sciences quite differently. Indeed, postmodernism questioned the search for a single unified, coherent meaning. It extended the critique of the idea of a universal truth to challenge the hermeneutic belief in the existence of an identifiable, single historical spirit and meanings. It further labelled the attempt to explain and delineate a distinct identity as being synonymous with the quest for foundations and essences. Consequently, while forsaking foundationalist languages, postmodernism stressed absolute contingency of the self, language and community.

V

Hermeneutic philosophy had questioned the idea of an abstract universal. In its place, it emphasized the historical nature of the subject and the presence of inter-subjectively shared meanings in society. The fact that postmodernism distanced itself from every aspect of hermeneutic understanding is significant not only for recognizing the distinctiveness of postmodernism, but also for comprehending the implications of this new ism for the study of social sciences.

Both Dilthey and Wittgenstein had acknowledged the presence of multiple meanings. They maintained that words acquire different meanings in different language-games and situations. The diversity of contexts imbues words with different meanings, and reference to these specific historical moments manifests this plurality of meanings. Thus, for them, words were multivocal insofar as meanings were context dependent. Postmodernism extricates the idea of multiple meanings and gives it a new form. It refuses to link multivocity to the difference in the historical context of the author and the reader, and relates it instead to a conception of the text. In other words, postmodernism claims that words do not acquire different meanings by being placed in different contexts, rather, multivocity is embedded in them. To put it in another way, postmodernism decontextualized readings and argued that multiple meanings are a consequence of the nature of the graphic sign. Just as the signifier is not exhausted by any signified, a word is also not reducible to any one meaning. As a text it is open to infinite new readings, even from within the same social and historical world.

By dissociating meanings from contexts, postmodernism allows for a free play of meanings. It gives the reader unrestricted freedom to interpret and create meanings, but at the same time, it also leaves the door wide open for epistemological relativism. Since multivocity is intrinsic to the text, all readings acquire the same status. That is, they was all equally valid and it is no longer possible to consider the adequacy of a particular interpretation. In fact, as we noted earlier, postmodernists maintain that questions of adequacy should not be raised because they are formulated in the vocabulary of represent-ation, and that is itself unacceptable.[45]

[45] R. Rorty, 1986 (a), op. cit.

Further, since reading is no longer concerned with the questions addressed by the author, or the central argument of the text, readers are left free to extract or isolate a segment of the text and weave the entire interpretation around it. In other words, reading is now unconstrained by the limitations imposed by the other aspects of the text. Thus, within the postmodern framework, multivocity comes to be equated with *equivocality* and no distinction is made between the two. As a floating signifier the text can take on almost any meaning and ' . . . the fact that a term can be used differently in two separate contexts, but with a clear and unquestionable meaning in each'[46] is itself questioned. Thus, plurality or multivocity that stems from the nature of the sign results in unmitigated relativism and rules out any discussion of the adequacy of the reading and interpretation.

In political struggles, the notion of plurality is frequently associated with difference, and this allows for a discussion of the diverse and plural sites of marginalization and oppression in society, plural subject identities and plural projects of emancipation. However, when difference becomes the sole criterion of interpretation and is dissociated from historical and cultural contexts, it dissolves into equivocality. It allows the sign to delink itself from the structured whole, erases its history, and allows it to take on almost any meaning. It is this transition from multivocality to equivocality that poses serious difficulties in the study of human sciences.

Gadamer had questioned Dilthey's hermeneutic method on the ground that it ignored the historicity of the reader. According to him, Dilthey erred in assuming that the reader could transcend his own historical world and reconstruct the life of the other. Further, Dilthey, like the positivists, reaffirmed the dichotomy between the subject and the object. Postmodernism affirmed this assessment of hermeneutic method. It rejected hermeneutic contextualiaztion, but instead of alluding to the conditions of understanding, it associated historical reconstruction as a way of 'fixing' meaning. In other words, postmodernism opposed historical reading on the ground that it predetermines meaning. In making this argument, it related its own anti-foundational agenda with anti-determinism.

---

[46] E. Laclau, 1990, op. cit., p. 29.

Previously, the critics of historical determinism had challenged the existence of invariable laws of historical development and spoken instead of the overdetermined nature of historical situations. They had argued that various coexisting structures — each capable of producing a particular effect — may in conjunction with each other generate an effect (event) that was neither predetermined nor attributable in advance to the existence/of a dominant structure. Similarly, variables that are individually insignificant may in association with each other yield a result that is completely at variance with our general expectations. Both these arguments hinted at the improbability of predicting with certainty what might happen. They provided space for human intervention and effect variation. However, in doing so, they did not doubt the existence of a structured pattern of interaction among these diverse variables, nor did they doubt the ability of a particular structure to generate a specific effect. What was challenged was the conclusion that the existence and preponderance of a particular structure would necessarily produce a given, predetermined effect. Postmodernism, on their hand, enunciates its own idea of non-determinism by arguing that texts are necessarily ambiguous, incoherent and incomplete. In other words, instead of alluding to overdetermined nature of structures, it questions the very idea of structure and patterned regularity.

This conception emerges most clearly in the writings of Laclau. Pointing to the ambiguity and incompleteness of the structure, he says that these attributes are 'not the result of the empirical impossibility of its specific coherence being fulfilled, but as something which "works" within the structure from the beginning.'[47] Further, ambiguity and indeterminacy arise ' . . . because the clarity of that context has not been achieved and the term does not manage to take on a definite sense as a result'.[48] In other words, for postmodernists like Laclau, the context itself lacks determination. That is, it is characterized by unstable relationships and absence of patterned regularity. This idea of ambiguous and 'undecidable' structures and 'unstable relationships',[49] rejects *tout court*, the idea of a structure.

The concept of *differance* also reaffirms this perspective. Insofar as

[47] Ibid., p. 28.
[48] Ibid.
[49] Ibid., p. 30.

'*differance* is the name we might give to the "active", moving discord of different forces, and of difference of forces . . .',[50] it makes salient the continuous and simultaneous presence of an otherness within. At the ontological plane, this conception of *differance* places an unbridgeable distance between Being and beings: that is, it undermines both the idea of an originating unity and a self-identical, coherent presence. At the epistemological plane, it suggests that meanings are deferred, delayed and disseminated: that is, they are never exhausted 'in the present of its inscription'.[51] The possibility of recovering new meanings of texts by 'inscribing or grafting it into other chains'[52] demonstrates the incompleteness, and with it, the validity of all readings. Further, since *differance* stands for 'not being identical' and 'being other', it places incoherence and ambiguity at the centre of *all* texts and readings.

The notion of incoherent and ambiguous structures has serious implications for the study of human sciences as it rules out explanations, however incomplete, partial or limited they might be. If structures are incoherent and their relationship with other structures irregular and ambiguous, then we cannot even theoretically associate effect with a particular structure. Hence, even *post-hoc* retrospective explanations become inconceivable in this rendering of the anti-foundational agenda. As such, all attempts to identify a coherent structure or its necessary attributes and determinate relationships are suspect within postmodernism; in fact they are avoided because they are also aimed at 'fixing' or determining meaning. Insofar as explanations require that we theoretically and temporarily close off what in reality is an 'open' system, there is no room for them in the postmodern agenda. Postmodernism is opposed to the introduction of every kind of closure, even a methodologically postulated temporary closure. Consequently, indeterminacy that was, for the critics of historical determinism, an attribute of ontological existence, now becomes a feature of epistemological enquiry.

The association of difference and plurality with indeterminacy and ambiguity gives a distinctive character to postmodernist anti-foundationalism, and, as observed earlier, the affirmation of

[50] J. Derrida, 1982, op. cit., p. 18.
[51] Ibid., p. 317.
[52] Ibid.

indeterminacy, incoherence and contingency undermines both explanation and systematic enquiry. Its critique of unified entities questions not only the notion of a unified society and a systematic whole, but also that of a unified subject/process/event, possessing a determinate form and identity. In addition, postmodernism views as suspect all attempts to transcend the particular and the ephemeral. The desire to pen down something which does not merely apply to one person once, was thus completely dammed (Rorty 1986b). In its place particularity, or more accurately, singularity is cherished and characterised as being the 'other' of foundationalist philosophy. The obsession with uniqueness and singularity delegitimises the search for generalisations and severely constrains the subject by trapping it in the momentary and the ephemeral. The subject, focussing on the 'here' and 'now', and forgetful of its own history, can, however, hardly be expected to distance herself from her inherited conceptions.

Thus, the concepts associated with postmodernist anti-foundationalism postulate a conception of self and society that raises serious problems. The postmodern defence of indeterminacy and incoherence makes schizophrenia the norm of everyday life. And its denial of narrative continuity and understanding jeopardises both social life and social interaction. In fact it places the social and the societal under erasure. 'The social', it suggests, 'only exists as the vain attempt to institute that impossible object: society'.[53] In the absence of the social, what remains is an aggregate of 'centreless individuals'.

Derrida's delegitimation of the study of 'origins' and historically contextualised analyses of meanings is thus supplemented by a denial of the social and an interrogation of both structure and system. This together with the mistrust of metanarratives, allows the postmodernists to legitimize the study of the particular in itself. The study of the event as an evanescent 'one off-happening'[54] without any history or follow-ups, structural or systemic constraints, become the order of the day. Given the disillusionment with Marxism, postmodernism encourages cultural studies which freely examine any and every cultural

[53] E. Laclau, 1990, op. cit., p. 92.
[54] Z. Baumann, 'Survival as a Social Construct', in M. Featherstone (ed.), *Cultural Theory and Cultural Change*, Sage, London, 1992, p. 30.

practice irrespective of its place in the system of signification that characterize a given society and social order. What is even more problematic is that it sanctions readings of these cultural practices in a vocabulary that is borrowed neither from the agent nor from that of the community. In other words, it allows complete freedom to the reader to construct the practice in an imaginative, bold and different way. The ability of the reader to place new images is now cherished more than any reflection of a determinate meaning. As a consequence, boldness of conjectures or readings alone becomes the distinguishing characteristic of postmodern enquiry.

VI

The value of postmodern enquiry resides primarily in its critique of those metanarratives that are woven around a dominant structure and a primary identity. Its reference to the internal 'other' points, quite perceptively, to the limitations of the metanarratives of the Enlightenment. However, its own anti-foundational agenda, postulated in terms of endless plurality, indeterminacy, incoherence and contingency, generates norms that vitiate social existence, communication, understanding and explanation. Although some of its adherents employ the idea of indeterminacy to argue that '*everything* is in human hands'[55] and in this sense, *created* not *discovered*, the absence of any discussion of structural constraints reduces contingency to the play of chance. Similarly, its celebration of indeterminacy offers a ready ground for a critique of the discourse of the state and the law since both seek to 'fix' meanings. However, the implicit subversiveness of these writings is once again undermined by the unqualified resistance of postmodernism to 'fixity'. The failure to grant even a limited space to determination (fixity) excludes the possibility of any performance and action. The postmodernist enthusiasm for indeterminacy ignores that utterances and performances of action involve a degree of closure. Even though situations are open ended, actions aim to give them a determinate end. Besides, actions emerge and are executed only when agents give a determinate meaning to situations. Thus, paradoxically enough, the postmodernist attempt to empower individuals actually

[55] Ibid.

vitiates consistent action and struggle. The postmodernist agents, aware of the incoherence and ambiguity of all structures, projects and life-worlds, can hardly be expected to commit themselves to political struggles, which invariably seek to fix meaning. Political struggle and action is further made difficult by the postmodernist belief that the end of dialogue is 'paralogy' — i.e. 'paradoxes, discontinuities and un-decidabilities of utterances'.[56] Since dissension rather than consensus is the motivating force in encounters and even 'consensus obtained through discussion' is seen as doing 'violence to the heterogeneity of language-games'[57] and by extension, to our freedom, there is no real possibility of achieving an agreement that can bind agents engaged in political struggle.

Given these analytical difficulties, we need to dissociate the negative movement from the affirmative agenda of postmodernism. As a critique of the metaphysics of presence and theories of correspondence, postmodernism provides perceptive insights but the concepts through which it delineates its anti-foundationalism are beset by a variety of theoretical difficulties. In particular, the association of anti-foundationalism with the presence of ambiguity, incoherence and relentless difference dissolves the textual object itself. More importantly, it undermines both societal existence and systematic, scientific enquiry. On the one hand, it excludes the possibility of offering even partial *explanations*, and on the other, it jeopardises communication and *understanding* in the social world. Consequently, it is necessary that we disassociate the two moments of the postmodern agenda. Only when we separate the postmodern critique of foundationalism from assertions about the incoherence and ambiguity of *all* texts, will postmodernism leave behind a legacy that can uniformly enrich the social sciences.

[56] R.C. Holub, *Jurgen Habermas: Critic in the Public Sphere*, Routledge, London and New York, 1991, p. 142.
[57] J.F. Lyotard, 1987, op. cit., p. xxv.

Bibliography

Achinstein, Peter. 1983. *The Nature of Explanation*, Oxford University Press, New York.

Adelman, Howard. 1974. 'Rational Explanation Reconsidered: Case Studies and the Hempel Dray Model', *History and Theory*, vol. XIII, no. 3, pp. 203–24.

Adorno, Albert, *et al*. 1976. *The Positivist Dispute in German Sociology* (trans. by G. Adey and D. Frisby), Heinemann, London.

Althusser, Louis. 1969. *For Marx*, Allen Lane, The Penguin Press, London.

Anisuzzam and Anwar Abdul-Melek. 1983. *Culture and Thought*, U.N. University and Macmillan Press, London.

Ankersmit, F.R. 1983. *Narrative Logic*, Martinus Nijhoff Publishers, The Hague.

——. 1986. 'The Dilemma of Contemporary Anglo-Saxon Philosophy of History', *History and Theory*, vol. XXV, Beiheft 25, pp. 1–27.

Anscombe, G.E.M. 1975. 'Causality and Determination', in E. Sosa (ed.), *Causation and Conditionals*, Oxford University Press, London.

Apel, K.O. 1972. 'Communication and the Foundation of the Humanities', *Acta Sociologica*, vol. XV, pp. 7–26.

——. 1977. 'Types of Social Science in the Light of Human Interests of Knowledge', *Social Research*, vol. XLIV, no. 3, pp. 425–70.

Aristotle. 1967 edn. *On the Art of Poetry*, Clarendon Press, Oxford.

Aronson, J.L. 1984. *Realist Philosophy of Science*, Macmillan, London.

Atkinson, R.F. 1971–2. 'Explanation in History', *Proceedings of the Aristotelian Society*, New Series, vol. LXXII, pp. 241–56.

——. 1978. *Knowledge and Explanation in History*, Macmillan, London.

Ausmus, H.J. 1976. 'Schopenhauer's View of History: A Note', *History and Theory*, vol. XV, no. 2, pp. 141–5.

Ayer, A.J. and P. Winch, eds. 1965. *British Empirical Philosophers*, Routledge and Kegan Paul, London.

Ayer, A.J. 1982. *Philosophy in the Twentieth Century*, Wiedenfeld and Nicholson, London.

Bacon, Francis. 1952 edn. *Advancement of Learning, Novum Organum*, New Atlantis, William Benton Publisher, Chicago.

Baier, A.C. 1970. 'Act and Intent', *Journal of Philosophy*, vol. LXVII, no. 19, pp. 648–58.

Baker, G.P. and P.M.S. Hacker. 1984. *Scepticism, Rules and Language*, Basil Blackwell, Oxford.

Bannet, E.T. 1989. *Structuralism and the Logic of Dissent*, Macmillan Press, London, Basingstoke.

Barnard, F.M. 1981. 'Accounting for Actions: Causality and Teleology', *History and Theory*, vol. XX, no. 3, pp. 291–312.

Bateson, Nicholas. 1976. *Data Construction in Social Surveys*, George Allen & Unwin, London.

Baumann, Zygmunt. 1978. *Hermeneutics and Social Science*, Hutchinson & Co., London.

Bennett, Daniel. 1965. 'Symposium: Action, Reason and Purpose', *Journal of Philosophy*, vol. LXII, no. 4, pp. 85–96.

Berger, P.L. and T. Luckman. 1976. *Social Construction of Reality: A Treatise in the Sociology of Knowledge*, Penguin, Harmondsworth.

Berlin, Isaiah. 1976. *Vico and Herder*, Hogarth Press, London.

——. 1980. *Concept and Categories*, Oxford University Press, Oxford.

Bernstein, Richard. 1979. *The Restructuring of Social and Political Theory*, Methuen & Co. Ltd., London.

——. 1982. 'From Hermeneutics to Praxis', *Review of Metaphysics*, vol. XXXV, no. 4, Issue No. 140, pp. 823–45.

——. 1985. *Beyond Objectivism and Relativism*, Basil Blackwell, Oxford.

——. 1986. *Philosophical Profiles*, Polity Press, Cambridge.

Bleicher, Josef. 1980. *Contemporary Hermeneutics. Hermeneutics as Method, Philosophy and Critique*, Routledge and Kegan Paul, London.

——. 1982. *Hermeneutic Imagination. Outline of a Positive Critique of Scientism and Sociology*, Routledge and Kegan Paul, London.

Bloc, Marc. 1953. *The Historian's Craft*, Vintage Books, New York.

Boucher, David. 1984. 'The Creation of the Past: British Idealism and Michael Oakeshott's Philosophy of History', *History and Theory*, vol. XXIII, no. 2, pp. 193–214.

Braudel, Fernand. 1980. *On History* (trans. by Sarah Matthews), The University of Chicago Press, Chicago.

Brodbeck, May, ed. 1968. *Readings in the Philosophy of Social Science*, Macmillan, New York.

Brown, R.H. and S.M. Lyman, eds. 1978. *Structure, Consciousness and History*, Cambridge University Press, Cambridge.

Brown, S.C., ed. 1979. *Philosophers of the Enlightenment*, Harvester Press, Sussex.

Brown, S., J. Fauvel and R. Finnegan, eds. 1981. *Conceptions of Inquiry*, Methuen & Co. in association with The Open University Press, New York.

Bubner, Ridiger. 1975. 'Theory and Practice in the Light of Hermeneutics —Criticist Debate', *Cultural Hermeneutics*, vol. II, no. 4, pp. 337–52.

——. 1981. *Modern German Philosophy* (trans. by E.Matthews), Cambridge University Press, Cambridge.

Buckle, H.T. 1930. *Civilization in England*, vol. I, Watts & Co., London.

Bulhof, I.N. 1976. 'Structure and Change in Wilhelm Dilthey's Philosophy of History', *History and Theory*, vol. XV, no. 1, pp. 21–32.

——. 1980. *Wilhelm Dilthey: A Hermeneutic Approach to the Study of History and Culture*, Martinus Nijhoff, The Hague.

Bunzl, Martin. 1979. 'Causal Overdetermination', *Journal of Philosophy*, vol. LXXVI, no. 3, pp. 134–50.

Burckhardt, Jakob. 1950. *Reflections on History*, George Allen & Unwin, London.

Burger, Thomas. 1977. 'Droysen's Defense of Historiography: A Note', *History and Theory*, vol. XVI, no. 2, pp. 168–73.

Burke, T.E. 1983. *The Philosophy of Popper*, Manchester University Press, Oxford.

Bury, J.B. 1970. 'The Science of History', in F. Stern (ed.), *Varieties of History from Voltaire to Present*, Thames and Hudson, London.

Butcher, S.H. 1951. *Aristotle's Theory of Poetry and Fine Arts*, Dover Publications, New York.

Butterfield, Herbert. 1969. *Man on his Past: A Study of the History of Historical Scholarship*, Cambridge University Press, Cambridge.

Butts, R.E. and J. Hintikka, eds. 1977. *Historical and Philosophical Dimensions of Logic, Methodology and Philosophy of Science*, Reidel Publ. Co., Dordrecht.

Carr, E.H. 1971. *What is History*, Penguin Books, Harmondsworth.

Cassirer, Ernst. 1950. *The Problem of Knowledge*, Yale University Press, New Haven.

——. 1955. *The Philosophy of the Enlightenment*, Beacon Press, Boston.

——. 1961. *The Logic of Humanities*, Yale University Press, New Haven.

——. 1962. *An Essay on Man: An Introduction to a Philosophy of Human Culture*, Yale University Press, New Haven.

Caws, Peter. 1967. 'Critical Study: Aspects of Hempel's Philosophy of Science', *Review of Metaphysics*, vol. XX, no. 4, Issue No. 80, pp. 690–710.

Cebrik, L.B. 1986. 'Understanding Narrative Theory', *History and Theory*, vol. XXV, Beiheft 25, pp. 58–81.

Chappell, V.C. 1963. 'Causation and the Identification of Action', *Journal of Philosophy*, vol. LX, no. 23, pp. 700–1.

Chisholm, Roderick. 1970. 'The Structure of Intention', *Journal of Philosophy*, vol. LXVII, no. 19, pp. 633–47.

Clark, Stephen. 1980. 'The Lack of Gap between Fact and Value', *Proceedings of the Aristotelian Society*, Supplementary, vol. LIV, pp. 225–40.

Cohen, M.R. and E. Nagel. 1957. *Introduction to Logic and Scientific Method*, Routledge and Kegan Paul, London.

Collin, Fain. 1985. *Theory and Understanding*, Basil Blackwell, Oxford.

Collingwood, R.G. 1938. 'On the So-called Idea of Causation', *Proceedings of the Aristotelian Society*, New Series, vol. XXXVIII, pp. 85–112.

——. 1965. *Essays in the Philosophy of History*, Texas Press, Austin.

——. 1976. *The Idea of History*, Oxford University Press, New York.

Conkin, P.K. 1974. 'Causation Revisited', *History and Theory*, vol. XIII, no. 1, pp. 1–20.

Croce, Benedetto. 1966. *Philosophy, Poetry and History: An Anthology of Essays*, Oxford University Press, London.

Dallmayr, F. and T. McCarthy, eds. 1977. *Understanding and Social Inquiry*, University of Notre Dame Press, Notre Dame.

Danto, A.C. 1954. 'On Historical Questioning', *Journal of Philosophy*, vol. LI, no. 3, pp. 89–99.

——. 1985. *Narration and Knowledge*, Columbia University Press, New York.

Davidson, Donald. 1963. 'Symposium: Action, Reasons, Causes', *Journal of Philosophy*, vol. LX, no. 23, pp. 685–700.

——. 1967. 'Symposium: Causal Relations', *Journal of Philosophy*, vol. LXIV, no. 21, pp. 691–703.

Derrida, J. 1976. *Of Grammatology*, trans. by G.C. Spivak, The Johns Hopkins University Press, Baltimore, Maryland.

Derrida, J. 1982. *Margins of Philosophy*, trans. by Alan Bass, Chicago University Press, Chicago.

DeVries, W.A. 1983. 'Meaning and Interpretation in History', *History and Theory*, vol. XXII, no. 3, pp. 253–63.

Dilthey, Wilhelm. 1976. *Selected Writings* (trans. and ed. by H. P. Rickman), Cambridge University Press, Cambridge.

——. 1976. 'The Rise of Hermeneutics', in P. Connerton (ed.), *Critical Sociology*, Penguin Books, Harmondsworth, 1976.

——. 1988. *Introduction to the Human Sciences*, (trans. and ed. by R.J. Betanzos), Harvester Press, Wheatsheaf, London.

Dovring, Folke. 1960. *History as Social Science. An Essay on the Nature and Purpose of Historical Studies*, Martinus Nijhoff, The Hague.

Dray, W.H. 1963. 'The Historical Explanation of Action Reconsidered', in S. Hook (ed.), *Philosophy and History: A Symposium*, New York University Press, New York.

——. 1970. *Laws and Explanation in History*, Clarendon Press, Oxford.

——. 1971. 'On the Nature and Role of Narrative in Historiography', *History and Theory*, vol. 10, no. 2, pp. 153–71.

——. 1980. *Perspectives in History*, Routledge and Kegan Paul, London, 1980.

Dreyfus, H.L. 1980. 'Holism and Hermeneutics', *Review of Metaphysics*, vol. XXXIV, no. 1, Issue No. 133, pp. 3–23.

Dreyfus, H.L. and P. Rabinow. 1982. *Michel Foucault. Beyond Structuralism and Hermeneutics*, University of Chicago Press, Chicago.

Ducasse, C.J. 1975. 'On the Nature and Observability of the Causal Relation', in E. Sosa (ed.), *Causation and Conditionals*, Oxford University Press, London.

Dussen, W.J. 1981. *History as a Science: The Philosophy of R.G.Collingwood*, Martinus Nijhoff, The Hague.

Elster, Jon. 1978. *Logic and Society*, John Wiley & Sons, Chichester.

Elton, G.R. 1967. *The Practice of History*, Sydney University Press, Methuen & Co., London.

Ely R.G., R. Gruner, W.H. Dray. 1969. 'Mandelbaum on Historical Narrative: A Discussion', *History and Theory*, vol. VIII, no. 2, pp. 275–94.

Ermarth, Michael. 1978. *Wilhelm Dilthey: The Critique of Historical Reason*, The University of Chicago Press, Chicago.

Fain, Haskell. 1970. 'History as Science', *History and Theory*, vol. IX, no. 2, pp. 154–73.

Fain, Haskell. 1970. *Between Philosophy and History*, Princeton University Press, Princeton, New Jersey.

Falk, W.D. 1963. 'Symposium: Action-Guiding Reasons', *Journal of Philosophy*, vol. LX, no. 23, pp. 702–18.

Feyerabend, P.K. 1981. *Philosophical Papers Vols.* I & II, Cambridge University Press, New York.

Foot, Philippa. 1972. 'Reasons for Action and Desires', *Proceedings of the Aristotelian Society*, Supplementary, vol. XLVI, pp. 203–10.

Forster, E.M. 1970. *Aspects of the Novel*, Penguin Books, Harmondsworth.

Foster, John. 1982-3. 'Induction, Explanation and Natural Necessity', *Proceedings of the Aristotelian Society*, New Series, vol. LXXXIII, pp. 87–101.

Frank, P.G., ed. 1961. *The Validation of Scientific Theories*, Collier Books, New York.

Gadamer, H.G. 1975. 'Hermeneutics and Human Science', *Cultural Hermeneutics*, vol. IV, no. 4, pp. 307–16.

——. 1979. *Truth and Method* (trans. by W. Glen-Doepel; ed. by J. Cumming and G. Barden), Sheed and Ward, London.

Gallie, W.B. 1964. *Philosophy and the Historical Understanding*, Chatto and Windus, London.

Gautam, S.P. 1992. 'Normative Structures of Human Actions and Causal Explanations', in Narlikar, Banga and Gupta (eds), *Perspectives from the Natural and the Social Sciences*, IIAS and Munshiram Manoharlal, Delhi.

Gardiner, Patrick, ed. 1959. *Theories of History*, The Free Press, New York.

——. 1961. *The Nature of Historical Explanation*, Oxford University Press, Oxford.

Gean, W.D. 1965-6. 'Reasons and Causes', *Review of Metaphysics*, vol. XIX, no. 1, Issue No. 77, pp. 667–88.

Geertz, Clifford. 1973. *Interpretation of Cultures—Selected Essays*, Basil Books, New York.

Genette, Gerard. 1980. *Narrative Discourse*, Basil Blackwell, Oxford.

Gibbons, M.T., ed. 1987. *Interpreting Politics*, Basil Blackwell, Oxford.

Giddens, Anthony, ed. 1975. *Positivism and Sociology*, Heinemann, London.

——. 1977. *New Rules of Sociological Method*, Hutchinson & Co., London.

Ginsberg, Maurice. 1934-5. 'Causality in the Social Sciences', *Proceedings of the Aristotelian Society*, New Series, vol. XXXV, pp. 253–70.

——. 1935. 'Explanation in History', *Proceedings of the Aristotelian Society*, Supplementary, vol. XIV, pp. 142–53.

138   EXPLANATION AND UNDERSTANDING

Ginsberg, Maurice. 1942. 'The Character of a Historical Explanation', *Proceedings of the Aristotelian Society*, Supplementary, vol. XXI, pp. 69–77.

Goddard, David. 1973. 'Max Weber and the Objectivity of Social Science', *History and Theory*, vol. XXII, no. 1, pp. 1–22.

Goff, J. Le and P. Nora. 1985. *Constructing the Past*, Cambridge University Press, Cambridge.

Goldstein, L.J. 1976. *Historical Knowing*, University of Texas Press, Illinois.

———. 1977. 'History and the Primacy of Knowing', *History and Theory*, vol. XVI, Beiheft 16, pp. 29–52.

———. 1986. 'Impediments to Epistemology in the Philosophy of History', *History and Theory*, vol. XXV, Beiheft 25, pp. 82–100.

Gooch, G.P. 1967. *History and Historians in the Nineteenth Century*, Longman, London.

Gottschalk, L. 1969. *Understanding History*, Alfred A. Knopf, New York.

Habermas, Jurgen. 1978. *Knowledge and Human Interest* (trans. by J.J. Schapiro), Heinemann, London.

———. 1984. *The Theory of Communicative Action, Vol. I* (trans. by T.McCarthy), Beacon Press, Boston.

———. 1989. *The Theory of Communicative Action, Vol. II* (trans. by T. McCarthy), Beacon Press, Boston.

Haddock, B.A. 1973. *An Introduction to Historical Thought*, Edward Arnold, London.

Hans, William. 1972–3. 'Meanings and Rules', *Proceedings of the Aristotelian Society*, New Series, vol. LXXIII, pp. 135–55.

Hanson, N.R. 1972. *Observation and Explanation*, George Allen and Unwin, London.

———. 1981. 'Observation as Theory Laden', in S. Brown, J. Fauvel and R. Finnegan (eds), *Conceptions of Inquiry*, Methuen & Co. in association with Open University Press, New York.

Harman, G.H. 1970. 'Knowledge, Reasons and Causes', *Journal of Philosophy*, vol. LXVII, no. 21, pp. 841–55.

Hart H.L.A. and A.M. Honore. 1973. *Causation in the Law*, Clarendon Press, Oxford.

Harvey, D. 1989. *The Condition of Postmodernity*, Basil Blackwell, Oxford.

Hegel, G.W.F. 1978 edn. *Logic: Being Part One of the Encyclopaedia of the Philosophical Sciences* (trans. by J. Findlay), Clarendon Press, Oxford.

Heller, A. and F. Feher. 1988. *The Postmodern Political Condition*, Polity Press, Cambridge.

Hellevik, Ottar. 1984. *Introduction to Causal Analysis*, George Allen and Unwin, London.

Helvacioglu, B. 1992. 'The Thrills and Chills of Postmodernism: The Western Vertigo', *Studies in Political Economy*, vol. 38.

Hempel, Carl G. 1959. 'The Function of Laws in History', in P. Gardiner (ed.), *Theories of History*, The Free Press, New York.

——. 1963. 'Reasons and Covering Laws in Historical Explanations', in S. Hook (ed.), *Philosophy and History: A Symposium*, New York University Press, New York.

——. 1965. *Aspects of Scientific Explanation and Other Essays in the Philosophy of Science*, The Free Press, New York.

——. 1968. 'The Logic of Functional Analysis', in M. Brodbeck (ed.), *Readings in the Philosophy of Social Science*, Macmillan, New York.

Herder, J.G. von. 1969 edn. *On Social and Political Culture* (trans. and ed. by F.M. Barnard), Cambridge University Press, Cambridge.

Hernadi, Paul. 1976. 'Re-presenting the Past: A Note on Narrative Historiography and Historical Drama', *History and Theory*, vol. xv, no. 1, pp. 45–51.

Hesse, Mary. 1980. *Revolutions and Reconstructions in the Philosophy of Science*, The Harvester Press, Brighton, Sussex.

Hexter, J.H. 1971. *The History Primer*, Basic Books Inc., New York.

Hindess, Barry. 1977. *Philosophy and Methodology in the Social Sciences*, Harvester Press, Hassocks.

——. 1990. 'Analyzing Actors' Choices', *American Political Science Review*, vol. 11, no. 1, pp. 87–97.

Hodges, H.A. 1949. *Wilhelm Dilthey—An Introduction*, Routledge and Kegan Paul, London.

——. 1976. *The Philosophy of Wilhelm Dilthey*, Greenwood Press Publishers, Westport, Connecticut.

Hollinger, Robert, ed. 1985. *Hermeneutics and Praxis*, University of Notre Dame, Notre Dame, Indiana.

Hollis, Martin. 1973. 'Deductive Explanation in the Social Sciences', *Proceedings of the Aristotelian Society*, Supplementary, vol. XLVII, pp. 147–64.

Hollis, M. and S. Lukes, eds. 1982. *Rationality and Relativism*, Basil Blackwell, London.

Holub, R.C. 1991. *Jurgen Habermas: Critic in the Public Sphere*, Routledge, London and New York.

Hook, Sidney, ed. 1963. *Philosophy and History: A Symposium*, New York University Press, New York.

Hookway, C. and P. Pettit, eds. 1977. *Action and Interpretation*, Cambridge University Press, Cambridge.

Hoy, D.C. 1978. *The Critical Circle. Literature, History and Philosophical Hermeneutics*, University of California Press, Berkeley, Los Angeles.

Hume, David. 1951 edn. *A Treatise of Human Nature* (ed. by A. Selby-Bigge), Clarendon Press, Oxford.

Humphreys, R.S. 1980. 'The Historian, His Documents and the Elementary Modes of Historical Thought', *History and Theory*, vol. XIX, no. 1, pp. 1–20.

Husserl, Edmund. 1965. *Phenomenology and the Crisis of Philosophy* (trans. by Q. Lauer), Harper Torchbooks and Row Publishers, New York.

Iggers, G.G. 1968. *The German Conception of History*, Wesleyan University Press, Middletown, Connecticut.

Iggers, G.G. and H.T. Parker. 1979. *International Handbook of Historical Studies*, Methuen, London.

Jameson, F. 1991. *Postmodernism, or, the Cultural Logic of Late Capitalism*, Verso, London.

Joergensen, Joergen. 1951. *The Development of Logical Empiricism, International Encyclopaedia of Unified Sciences*, vol. II, no. 9, University of Chicago.

Kant, Immanuel. 1973 edn. *Critique of Pure Reason* (trans. by Norman K. Smith), Macmillan, London.

Keat, R. and J. Urry. 1982. *Social Theory as Science*, Routledge and Kegan Paul, London.

Kim, Jagewon. 1964. 'Inference, Explanation and Prediction', *Journal of Philosophy*, vol. LXI, no. 12, pp. 360–8.

King, Bagda. 1964. *Heidegger's Philosophy*, Basil Blackwell, Oxford.

Kneale, Martha. 1971–2. 'Our Knowledge of the Past and the Future', *Proceedings of the Aristotelian Society*, New Series, vol. LXXII, pp. 1–12.

Kripke, S.A. 1982. *Wittgenstein on Rules and Private Language*, Basil Blackwell, Oxford.

Kuhn, T.S. 1970. *The Structure of Scientific Revolution*, University of Chicago Press, Chicago.

Kuhn, T. 1977. 'Second Thoughts on Paradigms', in F. Suppe (ed.), *The Structure of Scientific Theories*, University of Illinois, Urbana.

LaCapra, D. 1985. *History and Criticism*, Cornell University Press, Ithaca.

Laclau, E. 1990. *New Reflections on the Revolution of our Time*, Verso, London.

Lakatos, I. and A. Musgrave, eds. 1978. *Criticism and the Growth of Knowledge*, Cambridge University Press, Cambridge.

Langan Thomas. 1978. 'Searching in History for the Sense of it All', *Review of Metaphysics*, vol. XXXII, no. 1, Issue No. 125, pp. 37–52.

Langlois Ch. V. and Ch. Seignobos. 1966. *Introduction to the Study of History*, Barnes and Noble Inc. and Frank Cass & Co., New York.

Lee, D.E. and R.N. Beck. 1954. 'The Meaning of Historicism', *American Historical Review*, vol. LIX, no. 3, pp. 568–77.

Leibel, H.P. 1977. 'Review Essay: P.H. Reill's "The German Enlightenment and the Rise of Historicism" ', *History and Theory*, vol. XVI, no. 3, pp. 204–17.

Levy, David. 1981. *Realism. An Essay in Interpretation and Social Reality*, Carcanet New Press, Manchester.

Lewis, David. 1983. *Philosophic Papers*, Oxford University Press, New York.

Lloyd, Christopher. 1986. *Explanation in Social History*, Basil Blackwell, Oxford.

Louch, A.R. 1966. *Explanation and Human Action*, University of California Press, Berkeley.

———. 1967. 'History as Narrative', *History and Theory*, vol. VI, no. 1, pp. 54–70.

Lyotard, J.F. 1987. *The Postmodern Condition: A Report on Knowledge*, trans. by G. Bennington and B. Massumi, Manchester University Press, Manchester.

———. 1988. *The Differend: Phases in Dispute*, trans. by G. van der Abbele, University of Minnesota Press, Minneapolis.

MacDonald, M. 1933–4. 'Verification and Understanding', *Proceedings of the Aristotelian Society*, New Series, vol. XXXIV, pp. 143–56.

MacIntyre, Alasdair. 1967. 'The Idea of a Social Science', *Proceedings of the Aristotelian Society*, Supplementary, vol. XLI, pp. 95–114.

———. 1988. *Whose Justice? Which Rationality?*, Duckworth, London.

MacIver, A.M. 1947. 'The Character of Historical Explanation', *Proceedings of the Aristotelian Society*, vol. XXI, pp. 33–50.

Mackie, J.L. 1975. 'Causes and Conditions', in E. Sosa (ed.), *Causation and Conditionals*, Oxford University Press, London.

———. 1980. *The Cement of the Universe—A Study of Causation*, Oxford University Press, London.

MacMurray, J., A.C. Ewing, O.S. Frank. 1938. 'Symposium: What is
Action', *Proceedings of the Aristotelian Society*, Supplementary, vol. XVII,
pp. 69–85.

Madden, E.H. 1973. 'Scientific Explanations', *Review of Metaphysics*,
vol. XXVI, no. 4, Issue No. 104, pp. 723–43.

Mandelbaum, Maurice. 1938. *The Problem of Historical Knowledge*, Lime-
light Publ. Corp., New York.

——. 1977. *The Anatomy of Historical Knowledge*, John Hopkins University
Press, Baltimore.

——. 1984. *Philosophy, History and the Sciences*, John Hopkins University
Press, Baltimore.

Martin, Raymond. 1982. 'Causes, Conditions and Causal Importance',
History and Theory, vol. XXI, no. 1, pp. 53–74.

——. 1989. *The Past Within Us. An Empirical Approach to the Philosophy of
History*, Princeton University Press, Princeton, New Jersey.

Marwick, Arthur. 1970. *Nature of History*, Macmillan, London.

Mazlish, Bruce. 1963. 'Rational Explanations in History', in S. Hook (ed.),
Philosophy and History: A Symposium, New York University Press,
New York.

McCracken, D.J. 1952. ' Motives and Causes', *Proceedings of the Aristotelian
Society*, Supplementary, vol. XXVI, pp. 163–78.

McCullagh, C.B. 1978. 'Colligation and Classification in History', *History
and Theory*, vol. XVII, no. 3, pp. 267–84.

——. 1973. 'Historical Instrumentalism', *History and Theory*, vol. XII, no.
3, pp. 290–306.

——. 1984. *Justifying Historical Descriptions*, Cambridge University Press,
Cambridge.

McMurrin, S.M. ed. 1980. *The Tanner Lectures on Human Values*, University
of Utah Press & Cambridge Press, Salt Lake City.

McPeck, J.E. 1975. *The Context of Discovery in Context: A Closer Look at a
Positivist Dogma*, Proceedings of the XV World Congress of Philosophy, Sophia.

McRae, Robert. 1961. *The Problem of the Unity of the Sciences. Bacon to Kant*,
University of Toronto Press, Toronto.

Meiland, J.W. 1965. *Scepticism and Historical Knowledge*, Random House,
New York.

Meinecke Friedrich. 1972. *Historism. The Rise of a New Historical Outlook*
(trans. by J.E.Anderson), Routledge and Kegan Paul, London.

Merquior, J.G. 1980. *Rousseau and Weber*, Routledge and Kegan Paul, London.

Midgley, Mary. 1980. 'The Lack of Gap between Fact and Value', *Proceedings of the Aristotelian Society*, Supplementary, vol. LIV, pp. 207–23.

Mill, John S. 1978 edn. *Collected Works, Vol. VII: A System of Logic Ratiocinative and Inductive*, Books I–III (ed. by J. M. Robson), University of Toronto Press, Toronto.

Milligan, David. 1980. *Reasoning and the Explanation of Action*, Humanities Press Inc., New Jersey.

Mink, L.O. 1966. 'The Autonomy of Historical Understanding', *History and Theory*, vol. V, no. 1, pp. 24–47.

——. 1968.'Collingwood's Dialectic of History', *History and Theory*, vol. VII, no. 1, pp. 3–37.

——. 1970. 'History and Fiction as Modes of Comprehension', *New Literary History*, vol. 1, pp. 541–58.

Mokrzycki, Edmund. 1983. *Philosophy of Science and Sociology. From Methodological Doctrine to Research Practice*, Routledge and Kegan Paul, London.

Montesquieu. 1965 edn. *Considerations on the Causes of the Greatness of the Romans and their Decline* (trans. by D. Lowenthal), Free Press, New York.

Morick, Harold, ed. 1980. *Challenges to Empiricism*, Methuen, London.

Mukherjee, R.K. 1960. *The Philosophy of Social Science*, Macmillan & Co., London.

Murphy, M.G. 1986. 'Explanation, Causes and Covering Laws', *History and Theory*, vol. XXV, Beiheft 25, pp. 43–57.

Murray, M., ed. 1978. *Heidegger and Modern Philosophy*, Yale University Press, New Haven.

Nagel, Ernest. 1959. 'Some Issues in the Logic of Historical Analysis', in P. Gardiner (ed.), *Theories of History*, The Free Press, New York.

——. 1971. *The Structure of Science*, Routledge and Kegan Paul, London.

Nandy, Ashis. 1987. *Traditions, Tyranny and Utopias*, Oxford University Press, Delhi.

Natanson, Maurice, ed. 1963. *Philosophy of the Social Sciences: A Reader*, Random House, New York.

Neill, Edward J. 1968. 'Review of Carl G. Hempel's Aspects of Scientific Explanation and Other Essays in the Philosophy of Science', *History and Theory*, vol. VII, no. 2, pp. 224–40.

Nelson, E.J. 1963–4. 'Causal Necessity and Induction', *Proceedings of the Aristotelian Society*, New Series, vol. LXIV, pp. 289–300.

Nielsen, Kai. 1963. 'Rational Explanations in History' in S. Hook (ed.), *Philosophy and History: A Symposium*, New York University Press, New York.

Nielsen, M.H. 1981. 'Re-enactment and Reconstruction in Collingwood's Philosophy of History', *History and Theory*, vol. XX, no. 1, pp. 1–31.

Nowell-Smith, P.H. 1977. 'The Constructionist Theory of History', *History and Theory*, vol. XVI, no. 4, Beiheft 16, pp. 1–28.

O'Neill, John. 1976. *On Critical Theory*, Heinemann, London.

O'Sullivan, N. 1993. 'Political Interrogation, the Limited State and the Philosophy of Postmodernism', *Political Studies*, XLV, pp. 21–42.

Oakeshott, Michael. 1983. *On History and Other Essays*, Basil Blackwell, Oxford.

Olafson, F.A. 1970. 'Narrative History and the Concept of Action', *History and Theory*, vol. IX, no. 3, pp. 265–89.

———. 1986. 'Hermeneutics: Analytical or Dialectical', *History and Theory*, vol. XXV, 1986, Beiheft 25, pp. 28–42.

Ortega y Gasset, J. 1963. *Concord and Liberty* (trans. by Helena Weyl), The Norton Library, W.W. Norton & Co. Inc., New York.

Pandit, G.L. 1983. *The Structure and Growth of Scientific Knowledge*, D. Reidel Publishing Co., Holland.

Papineau, David. 1978. *For Science in the Social Sciences*, Macmillan Press Ltd., London.

Peters, R.S. 1952. 'Symposium: Motives and Causes', *Proceedings of the Aristotelian Society*, Supplementary, vol. XXVI, pp. 139–62.

Pflung, Gunther. 1971. 'The Development of Historical Method in the Eighteenth Century', *History and Theory*, vol. X, Beiheft 11, pp. 1–23.

Pompa, L. and W.H. Dray, eds. 1981. *Substance and Form in History*, University of Edinburgh Press, Edinburgh.

Ponty, M.M. 1974. *Phenomenology, Language and Sociology* (trans. by J. O'Neill), Heinemann, London.

Popper, Karl. 1966. *Open Society and its Enemies*, Vol. I, Routledge and Kegan Paul, London.

———. 1968. *The Logic of Scientific Discovery*, Hutchinson & Co., London.

———. 1975. *Objective Knowledge*, Clarendon Press, London.

Porter, D.H. 1981. *The Emergence of the Past*, The University of Chicago Press, Chicago.

Rabinow P. and W.H. Sullivan. 1979. *Interpretive Social Science*, University of California Press, Los Angeles, Berkeley.

Reill, P.H. 1975. *The German Enlightenment and the Rise of Historicism*, University of California Press, Berkeley.

Rex, Martin. 1977. *Historical Explanation*, Cornell University Press, Ithaca.

Rickert, Heinrich. 1962. *Science and History* (ed. by A.Goddard and trans. by G. Reisman), D. Van Nostrand Co. Ltd., Princeton, New Jersey, New York.

Rickman, H.P. 1979. *Wilhelm Dilthey: Pioneer of the Human Studies*, Paul Elek, London.

Ricoeur, Paul. 1974. *The Conflict of Interpretations. Essays in Hermeneutics* (ed. by Don Ihde), Northwestern University Press, Evanston.

———. 1976.' History and Hermeneutics', *Journal of Philosophy*, vol. LXXIII, no. 19, pp. 683–95.

———. 1981. *Hermeneutics and the Human Sciences* (trans. by J.B. Thompson), Cambridge University Press, New York.

———. 1984. *Time and Narrative, Vol. I* (trans. by K. Blamey and D. Pellauer) University of Chicago Press, Chicago.

———. 1990. *Time and Narrative, Vol. III* (trans. by K. Blamey and D. Pellauer), The University of Chicago Press, Chicago.

Rintelen, F.J. von. 1973. *Contemporary German Philosophy and its Background*, Bouvier Verlag Herbert Grundmann, Bonn.

Rorty, R., C. Taylor and H. Dreyfus. 1980. 'A Discussion', *Review of Metaphysics*, vol. XXXIV, no. 1, Issue No. 133, pp. 47–55.

Rorty, Richard. 1980. *Philosophy and the Mirror of Nature*, Basil Blackwell, Oxford.

———. 1980. 'A Reply to Dreyfus and Taylor', *Review of Metaphysics*, vol. XXXIV, no. 1, Issue No. 133, pp. 39–46.

———. 1986a. 'The Contingency of Language', *London Review of Books*, vol. VIII, no. 7 (April 17), pp. 3–6.

———. 1986b. 'The Contingency of Selfhood', *London Review of Books*, vol. VIII, no. 8 (May 8), pp. 11–15.

———. 1986c. 'The Contingency of Community', *London Review of Books*, vol. VIII, no. 13 (July 24), pp. 10–13.

———. 1989. 'Philosophers, Novelists and Inter-cultural Comparisons: Heidegger, Kundera and Dickens', paper presented at the Sixth East-West Philosophers Conference, Honolulu, July 31–Aug 11.

——— 1990. 'A Pragmatist View of Rationality and Cultural Difference', paper presented in Delhi, 26 Dec.

Roth, P.A. 1988. 'Narrative Explanations: The Case of History', *History and Theory*, vol. XXVI, no. 1, pp. 1–13.

Runciman, W.G., ed. 1978. *Max Weber, Selections in Translation*, Cambridge University Press, Cambridge.

Ruthrof H. 1981. *The Reader's Construction of the Narrative*, Routledge and Kegan Paul, London.

Ryan, Alan, ed. 1973. *The Philosophy of Social Explanation*, Oxford University Press, Oxford.

——. 1973. 'Deductive Explanation in the Social Sciences', *Proceedings of the Aristotelian Society*, Supplementary, vol. XLVII, pp. 165–85.

Ryle, Gilbert. 1980. *The Concept of Mind*, Penguin Books, Harmondsworth.

Sainsbury, R.M. 1979–80. 'Understanding and the Theories of Meaning', *Proceedings of the Aristotelian Society*, New Series, vol. LXXX, pp. 127–44.

Sayer, Andrew. 1984. *Method in Social Science*, Hutchinson & Co., London.

Schlegel, Friedrich von. 1979. *The Philosophy of History*, AMS Press, New York.

Schnaedelbach, Herbert. 1984. *Philosophy in Germany 1831–1933* (trans. by E. Matthews), Cambridge University Press, Cambridge.

Scholes R. and R. Kellogg. 1975. *The Nature of the Narrative*, Oxford University Press, Oxford.

Schutz, Alfred. 1967. *Collected Papers, Vols. I & II*, Martinus Nijhoff, The Hague.

Scriven, Michael. 1964.'Critical Study of E. Nagel's "The Structure of Science" ', in *Review of Metaphysics*, vol. XVII, no. 67, pp. 403–24.

Searle, J.R. 1983. *Intentionality*, Cambridge University Press, New York.

Sellitz C., M. Jahoda, M. Deutsch, S.W. Cook, eds. 1965. *Research Methods in Social Research*, Methuen & Co. Ltd.

Shope, Robert K. 1967. 'Explanation in Terms of "The Cause" ', *Journal of Philosophy*, vol. LXIV, no. 10, pp. 312–20.

Silverman, H.J. and D. Ihde, eds. 1985. *Hermeneutics and Deconstruction*, State University of New York Press, New York.

Silverman, H.J., ed. 1989. *Derrida and Deconstruction*, Routledge and Kegan Paul, New York and London.

Simmel, G. 1980. *Essays on Interpretation in Social Science*, Manchester University Press.

Simon, J.L. 1969. *Basic Research Methods in Social Science*, Random House, New York.

Skinner, Quentin. 1969. 'Meaning and Understanding in the History of Ideas', *History and Theory*, vol. 29, no. 1, pp. 3–53.

Skinner, Quentin. 1985. *The Return of Grand Theory in the Human Sciences*, Cambridge University Press, Cambridge.

Smart, J.J.C. 1964. 'Causality and Human Behaviour', *Proceedings of the Aristotelian Society*, Supplementary, vol. XXXVIII, pp. 143–8.

Sosa, Ernest, ed. 1975. *Causation and Conditionals*, Oxford University Press, London.

Spinoza, de Benedictus. 1963 edn. *Ethics*, J.M. Dent & Sons, London.

Stanford, Michael. 1987. *Nature of Historical Knowledge*, Basil Blackwell, Oxford.

Stegmüller, Walter. 1969. *Main Currents in Contemporary German, British and American Philosophy*, D. Reidel Publ. Co., Dordrecht, Holland.

Stephens, L.D. 1974. *Probing the Past*, Allyn & Bacon, Boston.

Stern, F.J., ed. 1970. *Varieties of History: From Voltaire to the Present*, Macmillan, London.

Stone, L. 1979. 'The Revival of Narrative: Reflections on a New Old History', *Past and Present*, no. 85, pp. 3–24.

Suppe, Frederick, ed. 1977. *The Structure of Scientific Theories*, University of Illinois Press, Urbana.

Sutherland, N.S. 1959. 'Motives as Explanations', *Mind*, vol. LXVIII, no. 70, pp. 145–59.

Sutton, Claud. 1974. *The German Tradition in Philosophy*, Weidenfeld & Nicholson, London.

Swain, M. 1978. 'Reasons, Causes and Knowledge', *Journal of Philosophy*, vol. LXXV, no. 5, pp. 229–49.

Synder, P.L., ed. 1972. *Detachment and the Writing of History: Essays and Letters of C.L. Becker*, Greenwood Press, Westport.

Taylor, Charles. 1971. 'Interpretation and the Sciences of Man', *Review of Metaphysics*, vol. XXV, no. 1, Issue No. 97, pp. 3–51.

——. 1980. 'Understanding in the Human Sciences', *Review of Metaphysics*, vol. XXXIV, no. 1, Issue No. 133, pp. 25–38.

——. 1980. *The Explanation of Behaviour*, Routledge and Kegan Paul, London & Henley.

Taylor, R. 1975. 'The Metaphysics of Causation', in E. Sosa (ed.), *Causation and Conditionals*, Oxford University Press, London.

Thompson, E.P. 1978. *Poverty of Theory and Other Essays*, Monthly Review Press, New York.

Thompson, J.B. 1981. *Critical Hermeneutics*, Cambridge University Press, New York.

Thompson, J.B. and D. Held, eds. 1982. *Habermas Critical Debates*, Macmillan, London and Basingstoke.

Topolski, Jerzy. 1980. 'Conditions of Truth of Historical Narratives', *History and Theory*, vol. XX, no. 1, pp. 47–60.

Toulmin, Stephen. 1953. *The Philosophy of Science*, Hutchinson's University Library, London.

Tranoy, K.E. 1962. 'Historical Explanation: Causes and Conditions', *Theoria*, vol. XXVIII, Pt. 3, pp. 234–49.

Trenholme, R. 1975. 'Causation and Necessity', *Journal of Philosophy*, vol. LXXII, no. 14, pp. 444–65.

Trigg, Roger. 1985. *Understanding Social Science*, Basil Blackwell, Oxford.

Tuttle, H.N. 1969. *Wilhelm Dilthey's Philosophy of Historical Understanding : A Critical Analysis*, E.J. Brill, Leiden.

Vendler, Zeno. 1967. 'Symposium: Causal Relations', *Journal of Philosophy*, vol. LXIV, no. 21, pp. 704–13.

Veyne, P. 1984. *Writing History : Essays on Epistemology*, Manchester University Press.

Vollmer, Kurt Muller, ed. 1986. *Hermeneutics: A Reader*, Basil Blackwell, Oxford.

Wallace, W.A. 1972. *Causality and Scientific Explanation. Vol. I*, University of Michigan Press, Ann Arbour.

Walsh, W.H. 1967. *Introduction to Philosophy of History*, Hutchinson & Co., London.

———. 1977. 'Truth and Fact in History Reconsidered', *History and Theory*, vol. XVI, Beiheft 16, pp. 53–71.

Warnke, Georgia. 1987. *Gadamer. Hermeneutics, Tradition and Reason*, Polity Press, Cambridge.

Weber, Max. 1968. *The Methodology of Social Sciences*, (ed. by Shils and Finch), Free Press, New York.

Wedberg, Anders. 1984. *A History of Philosophy, Vol. III*, Clarendon Press, Oxford.

Weinryb, E. 1975. 'The Justification of a Causal Thesis: An Analysis of the Controversies over the Theses of Pierenne, Turner and Weber', *History and Theory*, vol. XIV, no. 1, pp. 32–56.

Wells, G.A. 1959. *Herder and After*, Mouton & Co., S. Gravenhage.

White, H.V. 1973. *Metahistory : The Historical Imagination in Nineteenth-Century Europe*, The John Hopkins University Press, Baltimore.

———. 1975. 'Historicism, History and the Figurative Imagination', *History and Theory*, vol. XIV, 1975, Beiheft 14, pp. 48–67.

White, H.V. 1980. 'Droysen's Historik', *History and Theory*, vol. XIX, no. 1, pp. 73–93.

———. 1984. 'The Question of Narrative in Contemporary Historical Theory', *History and Theory*, vol. XXIII, no. 1, pp. 1–33.

White, J.E. 1971. 'Avowed Reasons and Causal Explanation', *Mind*, vol. LXXX, New Series, no. 80, pp. 238–45.

Willer, D. and J. Willer. 1973. *Systematic Empiricism*, Prentice Hall Inc., Englewood Cliffs, New Jersey.

Wilson, B.R., ed. 1970. *Rationality*, Basil Blackwell, Oxford.

Winch, Peter. 1973. *Idea of a Social Science and its Relation to Philosophy*, Routledge and Kegan Paul, London.

Windelband, Wilhelm. 1980. 'On History and Natural Science', Rectorial Address, Strasbourg, 1894 (trans. by Guy Oakes), *History and Theory*, vol. 19, no. 2, pp. 169–85.

Wisdom, J.O. 1976. 'General Explanation in History', *History and Theory*, vol. XV, no. 3, pp. 257–66.

Wittgenstein, Ludwig. 1981. *Tractatus*, Basil Blackwell, Oxford.

———. 1983. *Philosophical Investigations*, Basil Blackwell, Oxford.

Wogau, K.M. 1963. 'On Historical Explanation', *Theoria*, vol. XXVIII, Pt. 3, pp. 213–33.

Wood, Michael. 1972. 'Reasons for Action and Desires', *Proceedings of the Aristotelian Society*, Supplementary, vol. XLVI, pp. 189–201.

Index